Philosophical Works of Descartes

# Philosophical Problems of Psychology

# Philosophical Problems
## *of* Psychology

EDWARD H. MADDEN, *San Jose State College*

*New York*   THE ODYSSEY PRESS · INC ·

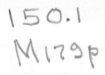

# Preface

IN THE following chapters I am mainly concerned with philosophical problems that arise in Gestalt theory, learning theory, *verstehende* psychology, psychoanalysis, and certain aspects of classical nineteenth-century psychology. Throughout I have the dual aim of clarifying the logical structure of explanation in psychology and of separating scientific and philosophical discourse where they have been inadvisably joined.

In this book I follow a convention in the use of quotation marks adopted by many logicians. I use single quotes around a word or sentence whenever I am saying something about the word itself, or the concept it represents— for example, 'finger' has six letters, or 'sister' and 'female sibling' have the same meaning. I use double quotes in the usual ways, as in direct quotations, in calling special attention to a word, and in "setting off" a word that is used uncritically or in an unusual sense.

I am indebted to many teachers and colleagues for the clarification of puzzles in the philosophy of psychology and for the encouragement so necessary to put together a book—even a small one. In the present work I have been aided particularly by Professors Gustav Bergmann, Curt J. Ducasse, John W. Lenz, and Ernest Nagel. I am also indebted to the editors of several journals for their permission to use material of mine which first appeared in their pages: "The Philosophy of Science in Gestalt Theory," *Philosophy of Science,* Vol. 19 (1952); "A Logical Analysis of 'Psychological Isomorphism'," *The British Journal for the Philosophy of Science,* Vol. 8 (1957); "The Nature of Psychological Explanation," *Methodos,* Vol. 9 (1957); "Psychoanalysis and Moral Judgeability," *Philosophy and Phenomenological Research,* Vol. 18 (1957). Even in these cases, however, I have revised the original articles. I owe most thanks, as always, to Marian Madden for discussing carefully with me all the problems in the following pages and for critically reading the whole of the manuscript.

E. H. M.

*San Jose State College*
*San Jose, California*

# Contents

Philosophical Problems of Psychology

## ONE

# Wholes and Parts

GESTALT THEORY includes a philosophy of science, and positions in epistemology, metaphysics, and value theory, as well as psychological notions. According to Wertheimer, Gestalt theory is "a palpable convergence of problems ranging throughout the sciences and the various philosophic standpoints of modern times."[1]* He also asserts that Gestalt theory was the result of concrete work done in psychology, logic, and epistemology.[2] In this chapter I will be concerned only with Gestalt interpretations of, and claims for, the method and structure of science in general.

Wertheimer and Köhler both regard the Gestalt view as a new interpretation of the structure and method of science insofar as it offers an alternative to the Newtonian or "analytical" interpretation of science. Wertheimer and

* For the notes to Chapter One see pages 125-29.

Köhler both reject the universality of "analytical" method, their thesis being that this traditional approach cannot account for some aspects of science which can be done justice only in Gestalt terms. Wertheimer's most formal condemnation of the analytical view of science and his thesis that there are areas to which it does not apply is to be found in his address of 1924 to the *Kantgesellschaft*.

It has long seemed obvious—and is, in fact, the characteristic tone of European science—that "science" means breaking up complexes into their component elements. Isolate the elements, discover their laws, then reassemble them, and the problem is solved. All wholes are reduced to pieces and piecewise relations between pieces.[3]

The word science often suggested a certain outlook, certain fundamental assumptions, certain procedures and attitudes—but do these imply that this is the only possibility of scientific method? Perhaps science already embodies methods leading in an entirely different direction, methods which have been continually stifled by the seemingly necessary, dominant ones. . . . Even though the traditional methods of science are undoubtedly adequate in many cases, there may be others where they lead us astray.[4]

Köhler takes the same position in saying that if problems of self-distribution in macroscopic physics were more familiar "the belief would not be so general that physics is under all circumstances an 'analytical' science in which the properties of more complex extended facts are deduced from the properties of independent local elements."[5]

In this examination of Gestalt philosophy of science I will first try to make clear the Gestalt views and then go on to construct an analytical terminology by means of which I try to show (a) that all legitimate distinctions of the Gestalters can be rendered in this language and (b) that Gestalters use such terms as "additive," "bundle," "interaction," and "field" both ambiguously and misleadingly.

### A. EXPOSITION OF GESTALT THEORY

Following the example of K. Grelling and P. Oppenheim we begin by distinguishing between W-Gestalts and K-Gestalts, the former term referring to a pattern or configuration which determines the nature of its parts and the latter term to systems of functional interdependence.[6]

Concerning what we have called "W-Gestalts" Wertheimer writes,

> There are wholes, the behaviour of which is not determined by that of their individual elements, but where the part-processes are themselves determined by the intrinsic nature of the whole. It is the hope of Gestalt theory to determine the nature of such wholes.[7]

*3*

A whole the behavior of which determines the natures of its individual elements is formally the negation of complexes the behavior of which is determined in the piecewise fashion. Wertheimer's schema for the latter kind of complexes follows:

> If I have $a_1 b_1 c_1$ and $b_2 c_2$ are substituted for $b_1 c_1$, I then have $a_1 b_2 c_2$. We are dealing essentially with a summative multiplicity of variously constituted components (a "bundle") and all else is erected somehow upon this and-summation.[8]

Any complex which transcends the nature of a summation or a "bundle" is a W-Gestalt. Examples are simple and numerous. The effect of transposing a melody is a familiar classic illustration. A melody made up of one series of notes is heard as the same as a melody composed of another series of different notes. In other words, a melody persists and is recognized even when played in different keys. According to the Gestalters it is this identification of melodies when the individual elements (notes) are different that supports the interpretation that the melody is not merely a sum of its parts but that as the whole it determines how the parts shall be heard. In addition Wertheimer discusses many factors, largely relational, which are intended to demonstrate the inadequacy of part-summation and the priority of wholes in determining perception. Such factors are likeness, nearness, common fate, objective set, closure, position and so forth.[9]

Turning to the K-Gestalt, a system of functional interdependence, we find that Köhler makes a basic distinction between microscopically and macroscopically organized physical states.[10] As a help in establishing the difference, Köhler refers to a network of pipes—three sections connected to the same inlet and outlet—through which water flows. He points out that the behavior of the water in each branch is not a local affair independent of any condition outside the particular pipe. If a valve in one pipe is closed the current will flow faster in those pipes remaining open, and if other pipes are added to the original three the current in the original ones will be slower. Knowledge of these interdependencies is contingent, of course, on one's observing the activity in a larger part of the network than one branch. If one considers activity within a branch pipe as well as what goes on in the rest of the network then the activity in the branch is seen to be relatively microscopic because it is not independent of outside occurrences and interferences. The entire network or, for that matter, any part larger than a branch is, relative to that branch, a macroscopic entity. According to Köhler, a certain kind of analysis of macroscopic entities is possible, a kind of analysis which tells us how events act within a macroscopic context. However, he points out, "More often . . . analysis is expected to give us *independent* elementary facts, the mere synthesis of which would yield the complex entities found in primary observation."[11] Analysis in this sense, Köhler concludes, is incompatible with the nature of macroscopic states.

The example of the pipes is a special case of "dynamic interaction" because the rigid channels permit interaction only at specific points. Köhler also considers the case of a single vessel with one opening for the incoming water and another for the outgoing water. How will the current be distributed in this continuous volume and how will alteration in the position of the openings affect the distribution? The important point in this case is that the current at each point depends more directly on the current at all points because the system is no longer restricted in its points of interaction. In these situations an equation for the steady distribution as a whole must be found if the equation for the steady flow at a point is to be found. Köhler contends that if such problems as these were more familiar "the belief would not be so general that physics is under all circumstances an 'analytical' science in which the properties of more complex extended facts are deduced from the properties of independent local elements."

## B. ANALYTICAL SCIENCE AND THE W-GESTALT

What one must do to refute the Gestalter's claim that certain aspects of science cannot be described adequately in analytical terms but must be described in Gestalt terms is to show that what the Gestalters say about relations, wholes, interaction, and fields—or better, everything they say legitimately about them—can also be stated in analytical terms. This reformulation in analytical terms of those features of science which the Gestalters emphasize and think that only they adequately describe might be called "methodological refutation." Semantically such a procedure amounts to a clarification of such terms as 'additive,' 'interaction,' and 'field.' More particularly, my methodological refutation must show that the features which Köhler thinks are unique to macroscopic situations are present already in what he calls the analytical parts of physics—i.e., where "the properties of more complex extended facts are deduced from the properties of independent local elements." I begin the refutation by describing in analytical terms the classical Newtonian problem of $n$ bodies.

I will assume that the classical Newtonian problem of $n$ bodies is known and will simply stress those features which are important for my purposes. We must distinguish two things at the outset, namely, description and explanation. First, there is the *configuration* of $n$ bodies and its initial and subsequent *conditions* at any given moment of time; second, there is the *law* which yields the values of the variables characteristic of one condition from those of an earlier or later condition (prediction or postdiction). All that pertains to the former—the masses and the position and momentum coordinates—constitutes a scientific *description;* all that pertains to the latter constitutes a scientific *explanation.* A W-Gestalt, which we have defined as a pattern or configuration, is a concept primarily relevant to scientific description; a K-Gestalt, which we have defined as a system of functional interdependence, is a concept primarily relevant to scientific explanation. Let us turn our attention first to scientific *description.*

Given a configuration of $n$ objects (mass points), $O_1$, $O_2$, . . ., $O_n$, the physicist knows from previous observations that each O is characterized by a number which is the value of an empirical construct called mass, which remains constant in time $\left(\dfrac{dm_i}{dt}\right)=O$. The mass of a physical object is thus an "index," a constant characterizer which is the non-configurational element entering into gravitational behavior. At least it is non-configurational (non-relational) as long as we do not push our analysis into a definition of mass itself. However it is not necessary to do this for our purposes because all we would gain would be a repetition of the situation we wish to discuss, repetition on a level more elementary in the sense of ultimate epistemological reduction but less suitable for our expository purposes.

At a particular time $(t=O)$ the physicist can obtain measurements which, as a class, determine the *condition* of the configuration at that moment. (The configuration itself is determined by the values of the masses.) The constructs measured are the positions and momenta of the $n$ bodies. These, we notice, are *relational* concepts; for the rest we assume that the distances and the time intervals out of which they are defined can be measured in some meaningful fashion without further analyzing these ideas.

The statement of these data at $t=0$ as a *logical conjunction* ("and" connection) of, say, $k$ sentences constitutes a "description" of the initial configuration. E.g., " (The mass of $O_1$ is $m_1$) & (The mass of $O_2$ is $m_2$) & . . . (The distance between $O_1$ and $O_2$ is $r_{1,2}$) & . . . & $S_k$." In stating this conjunction of $k$ sentences $S_1, S_2, . . . , S_k$, one is asserting the truth of all the sentences so conjoined; if at least one of the member sentences is false, then the whole conjunction is false. Such a logical product will constitute a description of the system and its condition at any time $t$.

In the light of this illustration let us now examine Wertheimer's thesis that "the whole is more than the sum of its parts," interpreting it at the moment as an emphasis on configuration or pattern, and let us see what are the possible meanings of it in analytical terms. In the analytical terminology of initial condition (description of the configuration at time $t_0$) and prediction of the condition at time $t$ (description of the configuration at time $t_1$), Wertheimer's thesis simply means that a description consists of several statements about physical objects, non-relational properties of such objects, and also statements of relations obtaining among them. Insofar as Wertheimer is emphasizing that statements of relations such as "*a* is to the left of *b*" are fundamental and not defined in terms of statements about objects or their properties, he is making an important point. In this case, however, his meaning is formulable in ordinary analytical terms. In fact we just did so formulate it. Only the classical materialists have tended to neglect the fundamental role undefined relation terms play in the description of nature.

In analytical terms another just and perfectly correct meaning can be given in the area of description to the classical adage that the whole is more than the sum of its parts. Consider a Newtonian system consisting of, say, six mass points. We can *conceptually* decompose this system into two sub-systems of three bodies each. One sub-system $(P_1)$ of the whole system can be described as consisting of the masses of three bodies $(m_1, m_2, m_3)$, their momenta, and their three distances. The remaining sub-system $(P_2)$ likewise can be described in the same manner. With descriptions $P_1$ and $P_2$ conceived as constituting the meaning of the term 'parts', the term 'whole' may be applied to a system $P$ composed of $P_1$ and $P_2$. Then it will be found that the description of $P$ is not simply the conjunction of the descriptions of $P_1$ and $P_2$ but contains *as further conjunctive terms at least some of the mutual distances between the bodies of the two parts of sub-systems.* In this sense it may be said that even in the realm of description the whole is more than the sum of its parts. This meaning of part and whole may of course be generalized. A "part," then, is a description of a sub-system of any group of entities. The description of the "whole" consists of the descriptions of all sub-systems *plus* the descriptive characters which indicate the relations between the sub-systems of the "whole" (in our example, mutual distances).

However, because Wertheimer's rejection of the "and" or "bundle" hypothesis indiscriminately includes both the "and" of description and the "and" of explanation and because he maintains that the latter—which would hold that the behavior of two systems $S_1$ and $S_2$ in spatial juxtaposition or partial overlap is the sum of the behavior of the two systems in isolation—is untenable, he consequently is insisting that the former—which is a logical "and" and simply means that the statements about objects, properties of objects, and relations between them are asserted together—is also untenable. The "and" of explanation does not in fact even have a clear meaning and should be rejected, but this does not impair the legitimacy of the logical "and" in description. To think that it does rests on a confusion between description and explanation.

That Wertheimer does consider the "and" of description untenable is implicit in his further consideration of the melody illustration. He considers the following explanation of this transposition phenomenon: one recognizes the melody in different keys because he responds not to notes but to intervals—relations—and *these* are what remain constant. Wertheimer, however, rejects this view because, he says, there are some cases in which the relations too are varied and the melody is still recognized.[12]

Wertheimer in this situation apparently is trying to discredit the elementaristic or summative view by showing the empirical inadequacy of adding new elements, relational ones, to the individual notes in an effort to account for the recognition of a melody despite a transposition. But even if it is true that a melody may be recognized even when the relations are not all maintained in transposition, it is not evidence detrimental to the legitimacy of the logical "and." In analytical terms I would simply say that the description of initial conditions, which are conjoined by the logical "and," is not complete. Let us amplify the notion of complete description in connection with the classical Newtonian $n$-body problem.

In the classical Newtonian $n$-body problem one says that a *complete description* embraces only mass points, distances, and speeds. But how does one know that the initial description is complete when only these constituents are listed? How does one know, for example, that the color of the bodies is not also a determining factor? Completeness simply means finding the empirical law; no *a priori* criterion for the completeness of a description exists. One must continue to add constituents to the initial description until he can state a law enabling him to predict subsequent conditions. The experimental check on this procedure is obvious. One observes several systems equated in all respects mentioned in the description. If the same results do not occur, then there is an "uncontrolled variable" that needs to be added. When it is discovered and added (by the logical "and") the description is complete.

Let us apply this analytical insight to Wertheimer's discussion of the melody. If indeed the relations between notes can be changed without altering the perceived melody, then we would say that adding relations to the notes still does not complete the description. If the constancy of response to groups of different elements (notes) cannot be attributed to something already contained in the description of the initial conditions we should (1) recognize the description as incomplete and (2) try to supplement it in one of the two possible ways: either add new basic data or derive new relations (e.g., ratios of ratios) from data already present. However there is nothing in this situation that justifies the belief that our account of description is in principle inadequate because it is too elementaristic.

The Gestalters would probably object at this point because we are consistently dealing with physical stimuli rather than with how the subject "sees" the stimuli. In our descriptions the statements refer to frequencies, to the ratio of frequencies, and to other matters of the "geographical environment." All we shall say now is that how a subject "sees" the stimuli is a matter of a lawful relationship between the subject's behavior and a complex stimulus situation rather than of the behavior *of* the elementary components *in* the complex. We shall return to this point in Chapter 3.

### C. ANALYTICAL SCIENCE AND THE K-GESTALT

We turn now to an analysis of the K-Gestalt and a formulation of its characteristic features in analytical terms. Given the values of mass, position, and momentum at time

$T_0$ the physicist can substitute these values in a formula—let us call it the computation rule—which will yield the values of these same variables at any time $t$ (that is, the computation rule yields the values of the variables as functions of the initial conditions and a continuous time parameter). The computation rule, of course, will be different when different numbers of objects exist simultaneously. The curve (law) for two bodies is different from the curve for three bodies and so forth. In the case of two bodies we have the law of a conic orbit; in the case of three or more bodies more complicated curves occur. In analytical terms any such empirical curve will constitute an "explanation." An explanation, then, is any function connecting subsequent descriptions of a system. When properties occur in any curve which do not occur in the curves of any lesser number of bodies, we will speak of this situation as *novelty* in respect to laws.

Let us assume that we have a computation rule for two bodies, so that a physicist could predict the future conditions for any given configuration of two bodies. Now this computation rule tells us nothing about the behavior of three or four . . . or $n$ bodies together. However, we can take the combination of three bodies, for example, and conceptually decompose it into sub-complexes or elements. The "elements" involved in the three-body configuration would be three configurations of two bodies each. Now we can apply our two-body computation rule to each of the elements separately. Next we discover inductively a rule which will produce the law for the three-body complex by combining in some definite manner the computation rules for the elements (in this example the rule is the so-called vector addition of forces). We will call this rule, which we discovered for predicting the behavior of a complex configuration out of the re-application of the computation rule to the "elements" of the complex, a *composition rule*. The general idea of the composition rule is to discover a single rule which will enable one to derive the computation rule for any given number of bodies. It must be emphasized that such a composition rule is just as much an empirical law, albeit independent of the empirical laws that obtain for the elementary configurations, as these laws themselves.

The success of this technique in wide areas of science is a fact. If one wishes to describe it by saying that science is "elementaristic," "mechanistic," or "additive," one is free to do so. Regardless of how one chooses his terms, though, it is important to note that 'additive' in this sense has a different meaning from the 'additive' whose meaningful and nonsensical connotations we tried to distinguish in the area of description. In particular, a composition rule is not a logical summation or "and" connection. (The terms "vector addition" and "vector sum" are rather unfortunate in this context and probably are among the causes of the confusion.) Nor does a composition rule, if it holds, imply that the parts of a whole independently go through the processes they would go through if they existed in isolation. Thus this "additive," "analytical," or "mechanistic" feature of science does not deny dynamic interaction of the parts of a whole. This point is sufficiently important to bear further elaboration and repetition.

As we have seen, Köhler stresses interaction in the sense that a change in one element causes alteration in all areas of a system. This is essentially what is meant by saying that a K-Gestalt is a system of functional interdependence. In analytical language, a prediction which holds for one set of initial conditions will in general not hold in *any* of its particulars if even *one* of the variables in the initial conditions is changed. The interrelations that actually obtain find their complete and exhaustive expression in the mathematical structure of the process law. Likewise, interaction is accounted for in the correct statement of the composition rule. In the case of planetary laws, if we know the Newtonian law for two bodies and for three bodies we still do not know *a priori* what the law for five bodies will be. This must be determined as a matter of fact. The deduction of the law of a complex from the laws of the elements is not a matter of linking together two laws by a logical "and." It is patently false to say that the composition rule is additive in the descriptive sense because in the case of planetary systems we would have planets with more than one orbit; planets in two places at once! A composition rule is *another* law, not a pre-existing rule for getting a logical product; this shows that Köhler is confused when he complains that in "analytical" science "the properties of more complex extended facts are deduced from the properties of independent local elements."

In summary, we see that both scientific description and explanation have several features which are rightly stressed by the Gestalters but which may be rendered in analytical terms. Moreover, by thus rendering them in analytical terms I have shown that some of these features are not quite what the Gestalters think they are and do not carry the implications which they think they do. The usual answer to this kind of claim is that the entire Gestalt thesis is not captured in these reformulation tactics, that the essence of the whole escapes the analytical net. We now turn to these "something more" aspects of the Gestalters' position.

## D. INTRINSIC WHOLES AND EXPLANATORY EMERGENCE

Wertheimer says that "there are wholes, the behaviour of which is not determined by that of their individual elements, but where the part-processes are themselves determined by the intrinsic nature of the whole."[13] If Wertheimer meant by this statement that sometimes the behavior of a subject toward a stimulus is (in part) determined by the whole or complex of which it is an element, then he is certainly correct. No psychologist, whether or not he is a Gestalter, would hold that a response to a stimulus $S_1$ is the same as the response to a stimulus $P$ of which $S_1$ is a constituent even if the subject has been given the "analytical" set of responding to $S_1$, which is thus once the whole and once a part of the presented stimulus configuration. In the analytical schema

(1) $S_1 \rightarrow R_1$
(2) $\underbrace{S_1 \text{ and } \ldots}_{P} \rightarrow R_2$    (organism "constant" in both situations)

The "and" in (2) is of course the logical "and" of description, so the total stimulus is different and there is therefore no reason why the response should not be different. Whether or not it actually is different is a matter of the law that happens to govern this particular situation. But when Wertheimer claims that the intrinsic nature of the parts is determined by their being in a whole, I must confess that I do not know what he means. Is not $S_1$, as an event, $S_1$ whether or not it appears alone or in conjunction with something else? The thing which may or may not change, according to conditions, is the *response* to $S_1$. This response is determined both by the elementary stimulus event and its context. But this event is the same in isolation or in context.

This discussion has concerned the "something more" aspect of the Gestalt doctrine in the area of description. In the area of explanation this "something more" aspect can be considered as a belief in *explanatory emergence*. Like other historical formulations of emergence the Gestalt formulation is not particularly clear. It usually takes the form of denying the possibility of predicting one set of characteristics from another. Koffka writes,

> Moreover, hydrogen occurs in nature in a form in which it is not composed of hydrogen atoms but of hydrogen molecules, each composed of two hydrogen atoms. Thus we have H, $H_2$, $H_2O$. This sounds like a straight molecular theory, but it is not anything of the kind. For H, $H_2$, $H_2O$ have all different properties which cannot be derived by *adding* properties of H's and O's.[14]

This assertion is misleading because scientifically no matter of fact by itself forms the basis for predicting the occurrence of another fact. *Predictability is always a matter of a set of conditions and a law or a theory in terms of which a future set of conditions can be predicted.* But let me characterize the matter in greater detail. First, Koffka is not contending in his chemical example simply that new laws arise with novel characteristics. Rather he is making the stronger claim (translated into my terminology) that *composition rules* or theories using them break down not only in the organic realm, as the vitalist contends, but already in the physical realm. This claim which I like to call *explanatory emergence* is not, however, a metaphysical assertion; rather it is the empirical meaning of the doctrine of emergence. Nor is the adequacy or breakdown of a composition rule an *a priori* matter. Whether or not a composition rule is adequate and to what extent it is adequate is a matter of scientific ascertainment. The allegedly "novel" and super-additive characters of the classical chemical illustrations, already favored by J. S. Mill, are by now in fact "mechanistically" explained in terms of quantum chemistry. That the Gestalters do not seem to realize the logic of this situation is borne out in Köhler's *Mentality of Apes* and other Gestalt literature in which the main contention is, in my terms, that empirical laws of insight are not only novel but also *must be* theoretical or explanatory emergents with respect to trial and error learning.

Any breakdown of a theory with composition rules at a certain level of complexity would be a case of explanatory emergence. The Gestalters, misled by their conceptions of "additive" and "analysis," as we have seen, claim that this level is already to be found in physics itself as well as in organic behavior. In spite of what I said above about explanatory emergence being an empirical matter, I do believe, given the complexity of organisms, that it seems at least *prima facie* more plausible that they are the kinds of wholes that resist explanation by means of composition rules. But even here, no doubt, the ultimate decision rests on scientific achievement or lack of it. (And certainly we do not seem on the brink of any notable composition law achievement in this area!) At any rate, it is plausible to conjecture that the Gestalt claim of explanatory emergence occurring already in physics has something to do with the halo with which the Gestalters have surrounded the notion of "field," since, as they say, Einsteinian mechanics is a field theory while Newtonian mechanics is "analytical," "mechanistic," and "additive." It is in order, then, that I say a few words about fields and the role this notion plays in Gestalt thinking.

### E. FIELD THEORY

Köhler always speaks of the necessity of *field theory* in psychology. Concerning field theory in perception and in its physiological correlates, he writes,

> By this (field theory) we mean that the neural functions and processes with which the perceptual facts are associated in each case are located in a continuous medium; and that the events in one part of this medium influence the events in other regions in a way that depends directly on the properties of both in their relation to each other. This is the conception with which all physicists work.[15]

Whether in physics or elsewhere, we can and must distinguish two meanings of the terms 'field' and 'field theory.' In its more general meaning 'field' simply designates a system of interaction; in its special meaning it refers to theories that work with a continuously spread medium and, accordingly, use the mathematical technique of partial differential equations. The planetary system, e.g., treated in the Newtonian manner, *like all scientific theories,* is a field theory in the first sense; but all scientific theories are not field theories in the second sense.

21

In order to understand better the second notion of field theory we will return to the *n*-body paradigm. Even though the concrete terms 'configuration,' 'conditions,' and 'objects' were used, we must not lose sight of the formal arithmetical schema—which we can call a calculus and which is coordinated with the empirical data. The system is in this case the finite and discrete ordered set of positive real numbers "corresponding" to the masses; a state is the finite and discrete ordered set of real numbers "corresponding" to the positions and momenta that determine a temporal cross section of the process; a process is always a continuous series of the states of the system as a function of time. So in the Newtonian case of *n* bodies a process is an ordered set of $6n$ functions of time. This discreteness and finiteness are characteristic of systems of interaction which are not fields in the second sense. A process schema is called a field schema in this second, narrower sense when either states or systems or both are not defined as finite ordered sets of numbers but as functions or ordered sets of functions spread out continuously through space like, e.g., temperature or electric field strength. That psychology has no field theory in this second sense is obvious when one examines the present state of this science. That it must be a field theory in the general sense is an analytical truth which results from its being a science; for every science is a field theory in the sense of interaction because, as we have seen, a change in one variable at time $t_0$ may alter all conditions at time $t_1$, and if $L_1$ and $L_2$ are laws of the parts of the whole in isolation it does not follow that '$L_1$ and $L_2$' is the law of the whole. The Gestalters have consistently blurred the distinction between the general and specific meanings of 'field.'

The reasons for this blurring may be found on at least two levels. Everybody familiar with the history of Western thought during the last century knows that certain specious semantic dichotomies have been erected upon the slender foundation of science half understood. Newtonian *mechanics* is not a field theory in the second sense; Maxwell's contribution to electro*dynamics* is a field theory in the second sense. And so, of course, is Einstein's general theory of relativity. Field theories, therefore, have prestige and supersede mechanics. "Mechanics," furthermore, is in our cultural tradition associated with "mechanistic," "elementaristic," and "analytical." And Wundt is "elementaristic" and "analytical" and, of course, the Gestalters are always in revolt against him.

On a different level, we can say that the Gestalters seize upon fields in the second sense because they feel, rightly or wrongly, that such systems share an intuitively clear "structural" characteristic with perceptual phenomena. In other words, this reason for their preference for fields in the narrower sense, like the distribution of charges on a conductor or in an electrolyte, is grounded in their principle of isomorphism. This kind of interaction that can be observed in such physical systems is peculiarly attractive to them simply because they believe its nature to be immediately translatable into terms of perception. As an example of this intuitivity one may cite the concept of a "good Gestalt." The left and right halves of a face, for example, are perceived as symmetrical although physically the face is more often than not only approximately symmetrical. As Köhler says, if a face is sufficiently near a standard condition of simple regularity, it will be perceived in a way which will eliminate its minor irregularities. "With regard to symmetry it will have 'too good' an appearance."[16] Then Köhler goes on, characteristically, to point out that macroscopic physical states like electric currents in electrolytes show exactly the same tendency. Such systems tend to develop in the direction of maximum "regularity" and "simplicity."

I hope by now to have carried out what I proposed as the task of this chapter.[17] What the Gestalters wish to say in their characteristic way about science can be said more clearly in the ordinary, analytical way which they reject as in principle inadequate. Some of what they actually do say in their own characteristic way turns out to be misleading. Thus, I believe, their claim that Gestalt theory is, among other things, a new philosophy of science is ill-founded.

*T W O*

# Isomorphism

THE CONCEPT of isomorphism plays a prominent role in logic and mathematics and accordingly it has received a good deal of historical and systematic analysis. The concept also plays a prominent role in some empirical sciences, most notably in the psychology of sensation and perception, where, however, it has received neither an adequate historical nor systematic analysis. Historically, analysis is confined to one or another type of isomorphism or is interwoven with other material so it does not form a unit. Systematically, analysis often is preoccupied with doubtful *a priori* judgments, pro and con.[1]*

After making preliminary statements about mathematical isomorphism, for the sake of subsequent comparison and contrast, I will provide what I take to be the elements

* For the notes to Chapter Two see pages 129-31.

of a historical and logical analysis of the concept of psychological isomorphism. The Gestalt variety of isomorphism, and its *a priori* epistemological justification, will figure prominently in this analysis.

### A. DIFFERENT TYPES OF ISOMORPHISM

The mathematical idea of isomorphism has two components. First, there must be a one-to-one correspondence between the elements of the two interpretations—or, as I shall also say, domains—which satisfy a set of axioms. Two sets of objects are in a one-to-one correspondence if they are paired off with each other so that to each element of the first set corresponds one and only one element of the second, and conversely. So one can say that the set of all mothers is in one-to-one correspondence with the set of all eldest children, whereas the correspondence between the set of all mothers and the set of all children is one-many. The second feature of isomorphism is that the different interpretations of an axiom set exhibit the structure specified by the axioms, although the interpretations may be very different in all other respects. Cohen and Nagel, for example, in their discussion of isomorphism give one arithmetical and one geometrical interpretation of a few axioms of projective geometry. Then they proceed to give the following general definition of isomorphism:

26

## Isomorphism

Given two classes $S$, with elements $a, b, c, \ldots$ and $S'$, with elements $a', b', c', \ldots$; suppose the elements of $S$ can be placed in one-one correspondence with those of $S'$, so that, say, $a$ corresponds to $a'$, $b$ to $b'$, and so on. Then, if for every relation $R$ [that is, in the axiomatic system] between elements of $S$ (so that, for example, $a\ R\ b$) there is a relation $R'$ between the corresponding elements of $S'$ ($a'\ R'\ b'$), the two classes are *isomorphic*.[2]

What Cohen and Nagel call the two relations $R$ and $R'$ are, of course, in my way of speaking, two interpretations in different domains of one relational predicate of the axiom system. But the question now arises, what has become of this notion of isomorphism in psychology?

There are several domains believed or claimed to be in some sense isomorphic, in which there has been great interest shown in the history of psychology. The first pair consists of the domain of stimulus events, on the one hand, and the domain of sensory events, on the other. The study of the relation between these two classes of events was referred to by Fechner as outer psychophysics as distinguished from inner psychophysics which concerns the relation of sensations to neural excitations.[3] However, the relation between the events of the two domains of outer psychophysics, as the classical psychologists conceived it, is not isomorphic in the full sense; at best it could be said that some classical psychologists proceeded on the assumption of a one-to-one relationship between stimulus and sensory events. But it will have to be shown that according to more recent results even *this* frame of reference is over-simplified and is not borne out by the facts.

In the area which Fechner called outer psychophysics variations in the physical dimensions were found to be correlated with variations in sensory dimensions. As Boring has pointed out, the procedure of Fechner, Hering, G. E. Mueller, and others was to vary only *one* stimulus dimension at a time and to observe concomitant changes in a *single* sensory dimension. "Out of such analysis grew the false belief that every simple dimension of sensation is correlated to a simple dimension of the stimulus—brightness or loudness to energy, quality to wave length or frequency."[4] If it were true that each sensory attribute were determined by, or dependent on, a single stimulus dimension the sensory attributes and stimulus dimensions would be characterized as being in a one-to-one relationship. There is in this, besides the idea of one-to-one correspondence, also, of course, the idea of a causal dependency in that the physical event determines the phenomenal event. Such a one-to-one relationship could be asserted if hue were in fact dependent solely on wave length, brightness solely upon energy of light, and saturation upon mixture of wave lengths. However it has been established that some such correlations are not one-to-one. The basic fact is that some sensory attributes are dependent on more than one stimulus dimension, e.g., hue varies with wave length and energy as well. It is possible, then, to produce the same sensory character by different combinations of physical stimuli. The situation is further complicated where not only is there not a one-to-one causal relationship between physical and phenomenal events but there is not even the *same number* of stimulus dimensions as there are sensory attributes determined by them. Boring cites, for example, the study of S. S. Stevens on the attributes of tone. Stevens found that for a bi-dimensional stimulus (a tone having the two dimensions of frequency and energy) there are *four* sensory attributes—pitch, loudness, density, and volume.[5] (The Gestalters emphasize such cases of lack of one-to-one correspondence between stimulus and sensory response and conclude that something must be "added" in the organism in order to account for the response. This is their point of departure for speculation about what must "happen" in the organism.)

There are, however, other domains in psychology which are, or were, believed to be isomorphic in a *full sense;* that is, domains which, in addition to one-to-one correspondence, allegedly shared certain "structural" characteristics. The first pair consists of the domain of receptor events, on the one hand, and the domain of afferent neural processes entering the brain, on the other; the second pair consists of the domain of neural events and of phenomenal events. The first type of full isomorphism found its most important exemplification in certain nineteenth-century "nativistic" (i.e., non-learning) theories of space perception;[6]

the second type, usually called psychophysical isomorphism, found important exemplifications, in the nineteenth century, in the color theory of E. Hering and, in the present century, in the numerous theories of Gestalt psychology and epistemology.[7]

(i) The domains which supposedly are isomorphic in nativistic theories of space perception are retinal or skin stimulation and the excitations in the afferent endings in the brain (leaving out the complication of depth perception). Such "projection" theories generally held that there is a one-to-one correspondence between the two sets of excited points and that the spatial relations of the retinal image are preserved in some topological fashion in the afferent fibres entering the brain. Also J. Bernstein proposed that the processes in the sensory surfaces of the skin were projected by nerve fibres upon the brain in a similar manner. These are cases of real isomorphism because they include in addition to a simple one-to-one correspondence between points on the receptors and points in the brain certain topological relations exhibited in both sets of events. Such projection theories were physiological models, speculatively formulated, designed to account for the perception of space. I am not here concerned with the question whether such theories are, in fact, right or wrong. They have been held by respectable scientists and there is no logical or methodological objection to them. On the other hand, it *is* important to point out that projection theories alone would not constitute a "nativistic" account

of, say, space perception. In order for the spatially isomorphic domains in the first pair to account for space perception there must also be structural relations in common
between the domain of brain events and the domain of
phenomenal events. What I have in mind is this: the nativistic solution to the problem of how space is perceived
depends upon projecting the spatial relations of receptor
stimulation on to the brain, but in order for these patterns
of stimulation of nerve endings entering the brain to be
efficacious in giving rise to *perceived* space, an isomorphic
relation between the domains of central nervous events
and phenomenal events—psychophysical isomorphism—
must also be assumed.

(ii) Psychophysical isomorphism, both historically and
systematically, plays a most prominent role in the use of
the isomorphism concept in psychology. As I have indicated, Hering, and others, and also the Gestalters, pro-
pounded their various theories within the framework of
this sort of isomorphism. Their procedure, because of a
paucity of pertinent physiological knowledge, was to infer
from phenomenal experiences the nature of the correlative
physiological process. That is, *first* one assumes an isomorphic relation to exist between these two sets of events;
*then* he uses features of the phenomenal world to characterize certain physiological events—isomorphic with phenomenal experiences—which will explain these features.

According to Köhler,[8] the isomorphism to which Hering
and G. E. Mueller referred obtains between the "logical

abstracted" orders of experiences on the one hand and physiological events on the other. This "logical" aspect of Hering's and Mueller's isomorphism consists in this: if a sound of a given pitch is presented a number of times at different intensities, and the various presentations are ordered on the basis of loudness, their logical order may be likened to a straight line. That is, the loudnesses proceed from softest to loudest without reversal. On the other hand, if colors are arranged on the basis of hue, the dimension is "circular" in form—as in the color cone. The principle of isomorphism states, then, for Hering and Mueller, that if the underlying physiological events were examined for the properties corresponding to these attributes, these properties would be found to exhibit the same order, linear in the one case, circular in the other. These ideas on isomorphism were explicitly formulated by Mueller in several very general psychophysical axioms which were, as Boring says,[9] accepted universally if implicitly. They state, among other things, (a) that underlying each state of consciousness there is a concomitant material (psychophysical) process; (b) that for similar or different sensations there are similar or different psychophysical processes, respectively; and (c) that for changes of sensation in a certain direction there are corresponding changes in psychophysical processes in the same direction.

The "abstract" or "abstracted" aspect of the Hering-Mueller isomorphism on which Köhler insists refers to the ordering of events within a particular sensory dimension on the basis of certain relations (louder, brighter, etc.). In

such a situation the observer has a set to attend to a particular sensory attribute, say saturation, while the other
attributes—hue and brightness—are disregarded. Since
each stimulus gives rise to a sensation having potentially
all three attributes, the experience of saturation under
the conditions of the particular set is an "abstract" one
and the ordering of the stimuli on the basis of the one
attribute is in this sense an "abstract" ordering.

The principle of psychophysical isomorphism espoused
by the Gestalters is, according to Köhler, "more general
and more concretely applicable" than that of Hering and
Mueller.[10] To explain his meaning he considers the example of three white dots on a black surface. "This," he
says, "is also an order; but, instead of being of the merely
logical kind, it is concrete and belongs to the very facts
of experience."[11] The claim then is that *there is also an
isomorphism between phenomenally given relations, on
the one hand, and certain relational features of their
physiological correlates, on the other.* If the point is made
in this way one avoids at least the misleading suggestion
that the "logical" order with which Hering and Mueller
are concerned is not based on experience whereas the
Gestalt isomorphism is. The simple point must be made
that the sensory experience resulting from an analytical
set is just as much a fact of experience as an experience
without an analytical set. The "logical" or "abstract"
aspect of Hering's and Mueller's isomorphism is the subject's concentration on the topological relations of non-
relational characters—e.g., the series of directional grada-

tions. Köhler need not quarrel with this. All he needs to do is *add* that experienced relations have their isomorphic physiological counterparts. Accordingly, Gestalt isomorphism claims in the case of Köhler's dot paradigm that the underlying physiological processes "are distributed in a certain order . . . and . . . this distribution is just as symmetrical in functional terms as the group of dots is in visual terms."[12] In other words, in the physiological processes there must be something corresponding to the perceived betweenness of the middle dot. Köhler formulates this characteristic emphasis in three principles.[13]

I Experienced order in space is always structurally identical with a functional order in the distribution of underlying brain processes.

II Experienced order in time is always structurally identical with a functional order in the sequence of correlated brain processes.

III Units in experience go with functional units in the underlying physiological processes.

The terms 'experienced order' in principles I and II and 'units in experience' in principle III unfortunately do not capture all that is involved in Gestalt isomorphism. That is, if one interprets, as is natural, the terms 'experienced order' and 'units in experience' so that they apply to *experienced* relations or *experienced* units within a perceptual field, then it would not refer to and would not include cases of a relational but nonexperienced character such as the field character and the character of a system altering its own medium. Since it seems that these principles are intended to cover these cases, the situation is worth exploring in some detail.

To give an example of Gestalt procedures: they take perceptual phenomena such as stroboscopic movement, perceptual grouping of *stationary* objects, and reversible figure-ground phenomena as requiring the concept of *phenomenal field,* by which is meant that events or objects located in one area of the visual field influence events in other areas "in a way that depends directly on the properties of both in their relation to each other."[14] Now this field character of visual experience, by means of the isomorphic principle, sets a requirement for the brain processes: the brain processes must have a physical nature which meets this requirement. Consequently Gestalt psychologists say that we must assume that physiological processes have the nature of a macroscopic physical system capable of dynamic interaction of the kind they hold is characteristic of fields—and electrolytic processes, they believe, best fill this bill. It is clear in the case of the perceptual grouping of stationary objects that we can say that a subject has one perceptual experience when stimulus entities bear certain relations to each other (similarity, proximity, and so forth), whereas the subject will see a different grouping when one or more of the relations among the stimulus elements are changed. But it is also clear that immediate experience does not include the observation of the elements in one part of a group *as depending* upon the other elements in the group in the way, say, that the spatial relations of before and between are a matter of immediate experience. In other words, the field character is not itself either a qualitative visual datum or a relational datum *within* the visual field like 'between' and 'to the right of'—characters exemplified by particulars within the visual field. Rather it is from *two* perceptual responses to two different stimulus situations that one *infers* that all parts of a system or group are interdependent in the sense that alterations of any one stimulus element or relation will affect how all the other stimulus elements are seen.

Let us recall Köhler's dot paradigm in which a matter of immediate observation, the experience of *a* being *between* *b* and *c*, sets the requirement which is to be met by the physiological processes. One dot is seen between the other two and this relation is part of immediate observation in the same way that the whiteness of the dots is a matter of immediate observation. Köhler says that there must therefore be something in the physiological events to correspond to this visual experience of betweenness. He writes, ". . . our principle refers to the relation between concrete experienced order and the underlying physiological processes."[15] However, we can see in the case of the field character that it is not always (and in fact it is not usually) a concrete experienced order which sets the requirements for physiological processes. Consequently the dot paradigm is not universal in the sense that it does not cover all the kinds of relations which are supposedly shared by the two domains of phenomenal and physiological events. If its natural interpretation is given to the term 'experienced order'—that is, if it is interpreted to refer to experienced relations in the various perceptual fields—then it would not refer to a relational but non-experienced character such as the field character. In another place, Köhler himself indicates that the phenomena which set the field requirements are not matters of immediate experience. He writes that "We seldom experience much of the actual genesis of visual percepts, but we can observe what things or figures appear under different conditions of stimulation. . . ."[16] We could say, then, that the conditions which cause certain perceptual phenomena are located in the brain field but unlike the physiological correlates of these phenomena the physiological conditions themselves do not have a phenomenal counterpart.

*As a result of our analysis it would seem that one must interpret Köhler's term 'experienced order' to refer simply to the fact that he uses unanalyzed experience rather than analyzed experience as his point of departure for isomorphic speculation.* It is in this sense that Gestalters are correctly said to have a "phenomenological" approach to introspection in contrast to the analytical set required in the classical introspectionism of Wilhelm Wundt and in the isomorphic speculation of Hering and Mueller.

37

## B. A PRIORI JUSTIFICATIONS OF PSYCHOPHYSICAL
### ISOMORPHISM

The interesting question remains, of course, why anyone should accept the hypothesis of psychophysical isomorphism, whether it be the Hering-Mueller type or the Gestalt variation. One might, of course, argue that the assumption is justified because it is scientifically fruitful. Suppose, Köhler says,[17] that an empirical law in psychology [designated $R(A, B)$] is discovered. The psychological terms will have their counterparts in brain processes ($a$, $b$) and the functional relationship $R$ will be interpreted as $r$, in some form of physiological or physical interaction between $a$ and $b$ [$r(a, b)$]. The problem at this point is some specific determination of the nature of $a$, $b$, and $r$, in lieu of adequate physiological detail. Specific assumptions about $a$, $b$, and $r$ will give these processes a position within the "system of concepts with which the natural sciences deal." These assumptions will not only have the characteristics of $A$, $B$, and $R$ which the theorist had in mind when he selected the assumptions about $a$, $b$, and $r$ but also will yield "implications" as a result of their position in a larger structure of physical knowledge. *With deductive elaboration of these assumptions we find that we get further assumptions about the physiological processes, say $a'$, $b'$, and $r'$.* With isomorphism functioning as a return bridge, there should then be in the phenomenal realm $R'$ ($A'$,

$B'$). If such a law already has been found independently in psychology, then (i) its theoretical connection with $R$ $(A, B)$ becomes apparent and (ii) it acts as a "partial verification of our physiological theory." If no such law exists as yet in psychology, then an experimental situation must be contrived to test its existence.

I do not wish to guess how good or how poor the isomorphism hypothesis is from this viewpoint of scientific fruitfulness; but I do wish to urge, since the concepts of this hypothesis are not inherently unclear, that it will be uselessness, and not *a priori* argument about the philosophical untenability of isomorphism,[18] that will remove this concept from serious consideration, if it is to be removed at all.

Conversely, the isomorphic assumption cannot be established by *a priori* or logical arguments either. This conclusion follows from the fact that there are significant empirical alternatives, in specific explanatory contexts, which do not involve the isomorphic assumption. To see this point, let us compare, e.g., the two classical color theories of Hering and Young-Helmholtz. One of the points of departure for Hering's color theory is the existence of four phenomenally fundamental or irreducible colors, the so-called primaries—blue, yellow, red, green—in addition to achromatic black and white. This suggested to him that there are three visual substances in the retina —yellow-blue, red-green, and black-white—which can undergo chemical changes in two antagonistic directions from an equilibrium point. All hues other than the six phenomenally fundamental ones were assumed to result from various combinations of these processes, that is, the excitation of more than one process. One principle of the psychophysical isomorphism on which Hering is operating is thus that to the four phenomenal "primaries" correspond four physiological "primaries." As is well known, Hering's hypothesis can be fitted to a large number of data including of course the arrangement of hues in a topological circle. *However it is also possible to account for (approximately) the same range of facts by the speculative model of Helmholtz which does not involve isomorphism with respect to primaries.* For Helmholtz, unlike Hering, took as his main point of departure the physical facts of color mixture discovered by Newton. And since three properly chosen colors mixed in various proportions match all other colors, Helmholtz assumed that not more than three primary processes, in the physiological sense of 'primary,' are operative in the visual apparatus. (It is only fair to point out, however, that Helmholtz's model leads to a question which finds an immediate answer in Hering's, while this is not so in Helmholtz's model. This question is of course: which are the features that characterize the processes corresponding to the four phenomenal primaries? I do not know what answer, if any, the Helmholtzians have given to this question, nor is this important. For the logical multiplicity of possible answers, e.g., certain maximal-minimal properties in the distribution of the three Helmholtz primaries, is very great. But again in this answer there is no trace of isomorphism.)

Nevertheless, *a priori* arguments *have* been offered which allegedly establish the isomorphic assumption independently of the question of its scientific usefulness. Köhler, for example, offers the following argument.[19] The phenomenal field, he says, consists of two different sorts of percepts—percepts of things like tables, chairs, and instruments, on the one hand, and percepts of the self, on the other. The concept of objective experience refers to the whole set of thing percepts within the phenomenal field. Now the physicist using this objective experience has successfully inferred the nature of the physical events which caused it. If there were no basic similarity, no isomorphism, between objective experience and physical events, then, of course, one could not "infer" or "draw a picture of" the nature of physical events. However, the phenomenal world is more "closely related," both causally and existentially, to the physiological realm than the physical, so *a fortiori* these two realms must be isomorphic and one is able to infer from the nature of the phenomenal the nature of the physiological.

This *a priori* argument for isomorphic speculation is open to criticism because, in fact, no isomorphic relation obtains between the phenomenal and physical realms, or, more precisely, between the givennesses of perception on the one hand and the theoretical concepts of physics on the other. For example, where is the isomorphism in any precise sense of the term between the movements of molecules and the immediately experienced character 'warm' which one naïvely ascribes to physical objects? All one can say is: first, in theoretical physics the concept 'temperature' is co-ordinated to some function of the average velocity of the particles. Second, after the co-ordination of all thermodynamic concepts to various features of the particle model is completed one expects to derive the thermodynamic laws as special instances of the laws of mechanics by applying the latter to the model. Third, the only necessary requirement is therefore that the functional relations among the concepts of the model be mathematically the same as the ones between the corresponding concepts of what physicists call phenomenological thermodynamics. Fourth, it is not clear why or how an isomorphism in any precise sense need or does obtain even between the concepts of phenomenological thermodynamics and the elements of untutored perception. As to the two domains of physical objects and phenomenal experience, then, it is not only not necessary but in fact false that the former mirrors the latter in the way Gestalt epistemologists call isomorphic.

To elaborate further this important point, consider the phenomenal experience of color, on the one hand, and the physical events which give rise to it, on the other. On the basis of phenomenal experience the hues form a topological circle, represented in the color cone, in which there are gradual transitions from one hue to a neighboring hue and a doubling back of hues towards the one with which one starts. But what about the physical events which give rise to these experiences? Of course, no such "topological circularity" is to be found in the physical basis of light and color.

These arguments, it should be noticed, eliminate the basis of the whole *a priori* argument; and so it is unnecessary to explore the hazy notion of the phenomenal field being "closer" to the physiological than to the physical field.

## C. THE NATURE OF GESTALT EPISTEMOLOGY

Gestalt psychologists invariably formulate and defend their isomorphic assumption within the framework of an epistemological dualism, namely, representative realism.[20] Thing percepts belong to the phenomenal world; the theoretical concepts of physics and physiology refer to transphenomenal real entities which cause the percepts. As effects the percepts "represent" their causes in the transphenomenal realm. And, of course, the phenomenal and physical-physiological realms are isomorphic. I think the isomorphic assumption can be stated within the framework of any epistemological system and that it would be wise to state it in common-sense terms since this epistemological framework, unexamined to be sure, is the one in which scientists ordinarily operate. However, since the Gestalters believe that representative realism is the only correct way to formulate the isomorphism hypothesis, it is necessary, finally, to examine the nature of the grounds of their philosophical predilection.

Koffka says[21] that the difference between the phenomenal and physical realms is equivalent to the philosopher's distinction between appearance and reality. And indeed the subtance of Koffka's argument for the existence of the phenomenal—or behavioral—realm or "appearance" emerges clearly as the traditional philosophical argument from illusion, the function of which is to establish the existence of sense data or percepts as distinct from physical objects. According to the philosophical dialectic, in cases of illusion *something* is being experienced and inasmuch as it is not the object it must be a percept or, in other formulations, sense data. In terms of a classic example, I see a straight stick partly submerged in water as bent. My experience of "bent stick" may not have a physical counterpart but nevertheless I am perceiving something—sense data or percepts. In Koffka's terminology, my "behavioral" environment is "bent stick" while the physical stick is not bent. The next step in the dialectic is to extend the claim that we apprehend percepts, and not objects, to all experiences. And Koffka appropriately universalizes his concept of behavioral environment: "But every *datum* is a behavioral datum; physical reality is not a datum but a constructum."[22] And in cases of illusion he tells us that the organism is not acting in a behavioral environment only at the moment of illusion but that it has been acting in the behavioral environment all along.[23]

44

## Isomorphism

Koffka thus asserts that the particulars of awareness are always percepts and never physical objects, but how does he establish the 'always' and 'never' in his claim? In characterizing certain experience as illusory he is assuming the validity of some other experience by which the illusion is discovered. In order to universalize his behavioral environment, then, he would have to supply, as he does not, in this context, some second reason why the apprehensions in these cases of valid perception are still percepts.

Koffka and Köhler in other contexts, however, do try to justify the universalization of their sense-data or percept claims. The dualist, Köhler says,[24] is able to tell "an impressive story" in which a representative element is present not as a philosophical theory but as a matter of physiological fact: stimulus energy impinges on nerve endings; nerve energy is transmitted into the central nervous system; phenomenal experience results. In one place Köhler *appears* to realize that this does not establish his representative realism. He admits that one might easily object that the use of words like "objects" already presupposes the existence of a world which is independent of and represented by experience and that consequently his procedure is circular. This criticism is too hasty, however, Köhler continues, because the phenomenalist for example does not contend that such things as brains, nerves, and sense organs are "unreal" but rather insists that what is ordinarily known as a physical object must be *interpreted* as a phenomenal entity. He concludes, "They cannot, for such reasons, refuse to listen to the Dualist's report. As a report, then, . . . [physiology] is common ground for both the Dualist and the Phenomenalist."[25]

If we are permitted to put Köhler's argument in our own terminology then we could say he holds that "the impressive story" is something every philosophical position has to take into account but that this story does not establish epistemological dualism. In spite of occasional passages that seem to acknowledge this familiar philosophical dialectic, however, Köhler does not seem to appreciate what seems to me an obvious truth, namely, that no amount of empirical data, as collected and interpreted by science, can establish an epistemological position directly. For example, he writes,

> Epistemological Dualism holds that percepts cannot be identified with physical objects, because percepts emerge only after many events have happened between the objects and the organism, in peripheral parts of the organism and eventually in the brain.[26]

However, that "objective experience," or the world of thing percepts, depends upon such things as physical energy impinging on receptors and transmission of neural impulses is a matter of scientific fact, and in this sense having percepts is a matter of physiology and psychology. It is clear that a percept in this scientific sense is not what it is the percept of and that when you and I look at the same galvanometer we yet do not have the same percept. This argument, however, is irrelevant to an epistemological discussion. When a person points out that objective experience depends upon certain complicated processes in the organism he is asserting laws which belong to the body of scientific knowledge. In such assertions obviously one has already accepted what constitutes a valid basis of knowledge and consequently such assertions have no epistemological significance. Epistemologically the question is what constitutes the valid basis of knowledge irrespective of the causal genesis of that basis.

One might try, of course, to establish as a philosopher and by philosophical argument a representative realism and, within its framework, what has sometimes been called a causal theory of perception. However this sort of argument is much different from Köhler's point. What we have called the causal theory of perception would hold that 'This is $x$' is equivalent to 'This is caused by $x$' where 'this' refers to a sense datum or percept and '$x$' to a physical object. The essential point in such a contention is that the physical object that is singled out as the cause of what is immediately observed is not itself a matter of observation. In Köhler's discussion of the galvanometer illustration, however, the physical object and sense data are both aspects within experience and between which scientific correlations are discovered.

I conclude then that the Gestalt variety of representa-

47

tive realism, in which Gestalt psychologists present and defend their isomorphism hypothesis, not only does not bolster their hypothesis, but is itself philosophically dubious. The Gestalters at this point might well deny themselves the luxury of a philosophical position on the problem of perception and let their isomorphism hypothesis stand on its own merit.

# *THREE*

# Lawfulness

Is IT POSSIBLE to predict a person's response knowing only some physical or social stimulus or is it necessary to know how the person "sees" or "understands" this objective stimulus before predicting his response? This question has plagued psychologists, social scientists, historians, and biographers from the very beginning of their enterprises and radically different answers have been given to it. The Gestalt theorist says no and the learning theorist yes, and each supports his view with reasons of varying degrees of merit. I want to examine these different views of lawfulness and prediction and will suggest each is legitimate within limits and each goes astray when it lays claim to exclusive excellence. Finally, I shall be highly critical of the *verstehende* psychologists who, while they share the Gestalt view, introduce 'empathy' as an explanatory concept.

## A. THE GESTALT AND LEARNING VIEWS

On the Gestalt view, external physical and social concepts are useless in the explanation of human behavior. One cannot use them to help explain behavior because he does not know how they are "internalized"—that is, how the subject "sees" or apprehends them. On the other hand, if one does know how the subject apprehends them, then he is in a position to explain or predict behavior. According to Koffka, one explains behavior by referring to the "psychological" or "behavioral" environment, never by the "physical" or "geographical" environment.[1]* Koffka uses many examples, both anecdotal and experimental, to justify his point. Through a snow storm a man walks over what he thought was a snow-covered plain only to learn later that the plain was actually the frozen surface of Lake Constance.[2] Knowing the frozen lake fact would not make it possible either to predict or explain the traveller's response; knowing his behavioral environment is necessary for that. He cites also the case of Revesz' chicks which were trained to peck at the smaller of two objects.[3] When two physically equal segments of circles were presented to the chicks they pecked most consistently at the one which, to us, *looks* smaller. Koffka says we must assume that the behavior of the chicks was determined by a relation and, since this relation has no geographical isomorph, it must

* For the notes to Chapter Three see pages 131-36.

be present in the behavioral environment. Other evidence which, he believes, compels him to assume a behavioral environment are the so-called constancy phenomena, i.e., situations in which, say, the same perceptual response is made to different retinal stimulations and different perceptual responses are made to the same retinal stimulation.[4] In the former case, the behavioral environments must be the same and hence the same responses; in the latter case, the behavioral environments must be different and hence the different responses. All of the examples, Koffka concludes, lead to the same conclusion: in order to predict the behavior of a subject a psychologist must know the subject's behavioral environment.

Some learning theorists have objected to this Gestalt analysis as completely untenable.[5] The behavioral environment supposedly explains why a subject will respond in a certain way, yet one only learns what the subject's behavioral environment is by observing this response. The behavioral environment snow-covered-plain explains why the traveller walked over the frozen surface of Lake Constance, yet one only knows the former after the latter has occurred. Certainly this procedure is *ad hoc* and circular. I do not think this criticism will do, however. Even though one cannot predict the response from which he infers the subject's behavioral environment he can, knowing this environment, predict further responses of the subject. (Certainly he could predict the traveller's surprise and consternation on later learning the truth. Indeed, according to

Koffka's tale the traveller dropped dead on hearing the news!) Spence calls this sort of achievement the discovery of "response-response" laws in contrast to the learning theorist's "stimulus-response" laws.[6]

The learning theorist offers the following analysis of psychological lawfulness, in which, needless to say, the stimulus variables are physical or geographical (or social) ones:[7] $R = f$ (S, H, D, I). Take the characters 'S,' 'H,' 'D,' and 'I' to refer respectively to geographical stimulus, past learning, motivation, and individual differences; 'H' and 'D' being, at the present state of our knowledge, historically defined. ('D,' e.g., could be defined in terms of time of food deprivation, although this example should not suggest that 'H,' 'D,' and 'I' are always defined as functions of one independent variable; frequently they are functions of several or more.) Now if one knew a determinate function that relates the variables S, H, D, and I to the response R, and had different sets of values for H, D, and I with the same S, then he would be able to calculate and predict two different responses to the same physical stimulus S and thus *explain* 'how subject sees S.' It does not seem unreasonable to speak of the group H, D, and I as the "equivalent" of an allegedly irreducible behavioral environment because it is their different values which bring about the different responses, although strictly speaking the function involves values of all four variables (S included). I do not claim, of course, that all behavioral environments can be so explained in terms of stimulus-response laws; it is a matter of scientific success or lack of it —finding or not finding the functional relations, etc. However some "behavioral environments," as well as behavior, require explanations, and it is difficult to see how any light could be thrown on their production without some use of learning, motivational, and physical stimulus variables. The Gestalt theorists, on the other hand, insist that an S-R type of explanation is *never* possible and the puzzle is to explain this insistence. The Gestalters insist on it, we shall see, because they believe it is necessary in order to safeguard their tenets of psycho-physiological isomorphism.

The S–R type of explanation with its variable groups H, D, and I implies that learning and motivational factors are necessary for an adequate theory of perception. The Gestalters, however, are unwilling to admit this; they insist that perceptual groupings are "irreducible," that is, are prior to and independent of learning processes. They are, of course, willing to grant that perceptual organizations are modified by learning. Köhler writes that "Gestalt psychology holds that sensory units have acquired names, have become richly symbolic, and are now known to have certain practical uses, while nevertheless they have existed as units before any of these further facts were added."[8] E.g., Köhler writes that when we peer into the sky we see certain clusters of stars detached from their environment, Casseopeia and the Dippers, for example. "For ages people have seen the same groups as units, and at the present time children need no instruction in order to perceive the same units."[9] Then he goes on to argue against the Wundtian type of analysis through kinesthesis by pointing out that any "empiristic" (learning) explanation of visual organization in terms of eye movements simply *shifts* the problem of organization from one sense modality (sight) to another (kinesthesis) and does not *solve* the problem of organization itself. Moreover, as is well known, part of Max Wertheimer's famous article "Laws of Organization"[10] is devoted to anti-learning arguments of this type. *But why this Gestalt antipathy to any learning explanation of perceptual grouping?* The answer lies in their hypothesis of psycho-physiological isomorphism, by which they hoped to provide physiological explanations of psychological laws and facts. According to the Gestalt version of the isomorphism hypothesis, the "field" characteristics of the physiological apparatus are reflected in the organization of the sensory contents to which they correspond. Now, since the physiological apparatus is structured or organized to begin with,[11] the sensory or perceptual contents must be likewise. They must come from the very beginning not as elements but in perceptual groupings. The learning theories of the associationists, or the intellectual acts of the students of Brentano, can only modify what is there already—like traces modify the brain field, according to Koffka. Perhaps one might say, the genetic problem of discovering what part of sensory organization is an elementary perceptual fact and what part is learned appears extremely important to the Gestalt theorists because they think their notion of isomorphism requires that certain perceptual responses or givennesses *not* be generated by learning processes. There is a three-fold answer to this Gestalt view:

1. The learning theorist, clearly, is not primarily concerned with ascertaining how many "groupings" are innate and how many are learned. But he is interested in finding by experimental procedure, first, the laws *under which any learning occurs* and, second, in determining if perceptual responses, or in Gestalt terminology, perceptual groupings, are among those that can be learned. The answer to the second question is, one may say confidently, yes.

2. There is no objection to accepting unlearned relational responses into a learning theory; it seems that, as a matter of fact, not all relational responses are learned. Such unlearned relational responses are taken into account in several learning theories, e.g., Hull's postulate of "afferent neural interaction." On the other hand, some rather elementary relational responses on whose "innateness" the Gestalters insist appear, at least in principle, derivable from non-relational responses by means of the laws of learning. Spence, e.g., in a much quoted article,[12] has derived certain transposition responses from the principles of generalization and the cumulative strengthening of habit strength.

3. *Relations or groupings once learned may well be phenomenally "given" or even introspectively irreducible.* To assert the introspective irreducibility of a givenness at a certain moment is one thing; to say that it has, or has not,

been learned in a certain manner is another thing. The Gestalters, however, in their anxiety to protect the irreducibility of perceptual groupings, and since they blur the two notions, insist, in effect, on irreducibility in both senses, 'unanalyzable' and 'unlearned,' when, in truth, for the sake of their isomorphism, they need insist on the irreducibility of perceptual groupings only in the first sense.

The Gestalters' lack of clarity about the two senses of 'irreducible' can be explained, I believe, in terms of certain historical relations between Wundtian structural psychology and the new Gestalt psychology which rose in reaction against it.

For the Gestalt psychologists, a learning explanation of perception or "behavioral environment" cannot be right because learning theory is "elementaristic."[13] The first link in this verbal bridge between "learning" and "elementarism" is the Gestalters' identification of learning theory with "associationism." This connection between learning theories and associationism is of course justified; the English associationists, Ebbinghaus, and Thorndike all gave an important place to associationistic theories of learning and no others worth the name of a theory or explanation have so far been proposed. However, and this is the second link in the bridge, "associationism" means for the Gestalters also and mainly Wundtian associationism. And Wundtianism is "elementaristic" in the sense that it insists on the possibility of introspectively analyzing phenomenally given relations into non-relational elements.

Relational experiences, according to Wundt, can in this sense be built up out of non-relational elements, both sensory and affective. This is the hard core of Wundtian elementarism, and this is essentially the doctrine against which the Gestalters rebelled and on which, consciously or unconsciously, their whole thought is fixated. Thus because they are so anxious to safeguard the introspective irreducibility of relational givennesses they believe that they must insist on the unlearned nature of perceptual responses.

B. THE EXPERIENCE ERROR

According to Köhler, the correct formula for psychological lawfulness is this: receptor stimulation; organization of these stimuli by the central nervous system; and response to the product of organization.[14] Knowing only the receptor stimulation, one could not predict a subject's response; one needs to know how the subject apprehends or organizes the stimuli. Thus Köhler agrees with Koffka that the idea of behavioral environment is irreducible and indispensable, and from this standpoint he characterizes the S–R conception of stimulus as incorrect. Let us look into his argument in some detail.

Köhler proposes to label as the *experience error* the erroneous ascription of organization to a mosaic of receptor stimulation, e.g., retinal stimulation. "Physiologists and psychologists are inclined to talk about *the* retinal process which corresponds to an object, as though stimulation within the retinal area of the object constituted a segregated unit."[15] The facts are far otherwise, he believes. Say you see a sheep behind a fence. Now each element of the surface of the sheep and the fence reflects light independently. In this case two elements of the sheep's surface are no more related to each other than one of them is to an element of the fence's surface. "Hence, so far as retinal stimulation is concerned, there is no organization, no segregation of specific units or groups."[16] The autochthonous activity of the central nervous system is the organizing agent; its function, one might say, is to reorganize stimuli and thus recreate the relationships that were lost in the separation sieve of receptor stimulation. Or the nervous system may create relationships which do not even have a physical counterpart at all. In either case, the correct schema of lawfulness is this: receptor stimulation, organization of stimuli, and response to the product of organization.

How the S–R learning theorist goes wrong, Köhler thinks, should now be clear. He talks about the objective physical object as the stimulus for a subject. But this will not do, for the subject's proper stimulus is unstructured receptor stimulation which is turned into a structured stimulus by the central nervous system. Köhler writes that he once tried to convince a behaviorist that he should not refer to a female bird as "a stimulus" for a male bird because this way of talking ignores the facts of organization.[17] The behaviorist, however, Köhler continues, went on committing the experience error because he did not understand the importance of sensory experience for psychological theory. Moreover, Köhler says,[18] we are now in a position to see why the behaviorist's stimulus-response formula of lawfulness is mistaken, plausible as it might seem at first glance. The behaviorist simply uses the term stimulus in a loose fashion, applying it to an objective physical object which has already been perceptually structured.

The reply to Köhler's view is four-fold:

1. There is a deep lying philosophical confusion in this argument. Köhler, it would seem, forgets that in building the science of psychology one can use relational terms in the description of a stimulus without first accounting, within this science, for the perception of relations. We have here a confusion between a scientific "causal" explanation and the question of what is included in the level of undefined terms in scientific definition. Köhler confusedly thinks that one must generate the relational terms of the latter by a causal analysis before one may use them in describing a distal object as stimulus. When one realizes that relational terms are included among the undefined concepts in scientific definition and so are prior to any scientific study of perception, the groundlessness of the argument becomes clear and the charge of circularity, which Köhler implicitly makes against the S–R theorist's construction, is seen to be unjustified. And likewise un-

justified is what appears to be the Gestalters' implicit idea of the referent of the symbol 'S' in the S–R schema. Influenced by the fixation on Wundtian issues and by the other ideas we are now discussing, they always think of the referent of 'S' as an unstructured, non-relational "element"; distally, a monochromatic patch on a projection screen in a typical sensation experiment, proximally, the local retinal excitation produced by such a stimulus. Nothing is farther from the truth. 'S' like the other variables in the S–R schema may stand for a whole group of variables, including relational terms.

2. In this argument the Gestalters claim that receptor stimulation, not physical objects, is the "proper" stimulus of a subject; and they insist that retinal mosaics, not whole "macro" objects, are the "real" stimulus of a subject. Thus the Gestalters decide on *a priori* grounds what must be the locus of a stimulus and the units of its size. In fact, of course, the choice of the locus of the stimulus, the choice of units of description, and the inclusion of relations in it is not a systematic issue. The units one chooses in defining one's variables and the locus of them depend upon what sort of law is wanted. No type of law in itself is intrinsically good, albeit one might want a certain kind of law for systematic reasons. (E.g., an S–R law might explain an R–R one but the reverse could not occur.) Ever since the downfall of Wundt the tendency in psychology has been toward the use of physical macro units in the description

of stimulus situations. If one believes that this is fortunate it is only because at the present stage of knowledge the choice of such units is as a matter of fact more likely to lead to the establishment of laws. Neither it nor the Gestalt alternative is to be rationalized on *a priori* grounds such as Köhler advances.

3. Köhler seems to say that retinal stimuli exhibit no organization. But clearly they do. Although retinal stimuli are discrete and independent, they do exhibit relations such as contiguity and similarity. These relations, of course, Köhler would call "formal" or "geometrical," not "functional"—where the word functional means dynamic interaction—and would depreciate their significance. But the point is this: Köhler does not explicitly point out that the lack of "functional interaction" is not identical with a lack of all organization; consequently when he writes that retinal stimuli have no organization there is at least the silent implication that no relations are exemplified in the proximal stimulus pattern to which a response can be learned. Hence the *non sequitur* that no S–R schema of the constancy phenomena can be devised.

Actually the various retinal stimulations due to one and the same physical micro-stimulus object do of course exhibit relational invariances to which the learned response may be made. Let us elaborate this matter within the framework of the S–R schema for explaining certain constancy phenomena.

Let us call S the physical stimulus object and let

$$(1) \quad \begin{array}{l} s_1', s_2', \ \ldots \ s_n' \\ s_1'', s_2'', \ \ldots \ s_n'' \\ \quad \bullet \quad \bullet \quad \bullet \\ s_1^{(m)}, s_2^{(m)}, \ \ldots \ s_n^{(m)} \end{array}$$

be the *m* patterns of retinal stimulations corresponding to *m* different "views" of S. In retinal micro terms the stimulus is in each case not one elementary entity but a group of such, as I called it before; and, let me repeat, a group that may and as a rule will include relational traits such as, e.g., the spatial relations between the patches of homogenous retinal stimulation.

Thing constancy is then expressed by the following schema:

$$(2) \quad \begin{array}{l} R_1 = f(s_1', s_2', \ \ldots \ s_n', X) \\ R_1 = f(s_1'', s_2'', \ \ldots \ s_n'', X) \\ \\ R_1 = f(s_1^{(m)}, s_2^{\ (m)}, \ \ldots \ s_n^{(m)}, X) \end{array}$$

The problem then is to find a function (complex relation) which remains constant for all the lines of (1). *Any* such functions can, by the logic of the case, serve as a cue for the macro response which, if verbal, may be thought of as "This is S." Which of the several possible functions of this sort is the actual clue is a matter to be determined by experimentation. To leave no possible doubt that there are such functions, consider the light waves coming from the same distal object. They give rise to different proximal stimulation, but they are all sections of the class of light beams which is reflected from the surface of the object. Inasmuch as the various proximal stimulus situations are all such intersections, there is a relational invariant to be responded to, like the ratio of frequencies in a tune.

4. Finally, Köhler and Koffka believe that 'S' can never be a physical stimulus but is always a perceived or apprehended 'S' because they are committed philosophically to a representative realism and thus acknowledge only mediate knowledge of physical objects. However, since their isomorphism hypothesis can be formulated in any epistemological system no particular one is *necessary* for it; and, as I have tried to show in the previous chapter, the grounds they advance for their representative preferences are a curious mixture of philosophical and scientific arguments.

### C. VERSTEHENDE AND EMPATHY

*Verstehende* psychologists who follow Dilthey and Spranger, phenomenologists like Snygg, and various other psychologists who specialize in personality studies take the same view as Koffka and Köhler about the irreducibility of 'behavioral environment,' and the uselessness of a physical stimulus;[19] but they eschew the physiological explanations of the Gestalters and use instead behavior maxims which supposedly give empathetic understanding of the other fellow's behavior.

Recall the case of the traveller who walked over the frozen surface of Lake Constance. According to Snygg and certain *verstehende* psychologists,[20] the external fact is useless in explaining the traveller's behavior; one needs to know he sees it as snow-covered-plain. Then a behavior maxim drawn from everyday life connects this "internalized" stimulus with his response and thus explains it. The behavior maxim in this case, of course, is that people take the most direct line of action to get out of unpleasant situations. For the traveller the apparent plain offers the most direct line of approach or shortest route to the light of an inn; hence he takes this route. While this maxim explains his behavior it is not yet clear what is "empathetic" about it. The point is this: a behavior maxim is not "discovered"; it is immediately experienced as an understandable relation.[21] Thus the other fellow's acting on it—which explains his behavior—is understandable too: I have an empathetic feeling for him. The empathetic understanding, finally, does not come simply from the capacity to experience explanatory relations but from actually having them; if understanding is to occur, one must not simply be capable of having the same motives as another but must actually share them.[22]

The inadequacy of the empathy viewpoint is indicated in the fact that it is neither a sufficient nor necessary condition for explanations in psychology. First, incompatible explanations of behavior are usually equally understandable so one needs another criterion besides understanding to determine which of the alternative explanations is correct. This criterion, of course, is objective observation and experiment. We can make the same point by saying that empathy indicates only possible but not probable explanations. According to Theodore Abel,

> When we say we "understand" a connection, we imply nothing more than recognizing it as a possible one. We simply affirm that we have at least once in direct experience observed and established the connection or its equivalent. But from the affirmation of a possible connection we cannot conclude that it is also probable. From the point of view of *verstehen* [empathy] alone, any connection that is possible is *equally* certain. In any given case the test of the actual probability calls for the application of objective methods of observation. . . .[23]

Second, empathy is not a necessary requirement for psychological explanation either. There is a whole series of subjects which are, for most people, increasingly difficult to understand empathetically. At the apex would be a person like Hitler, certainly a legitimate object of psychological study. That Hitler's hatreds and ambitions are "experienceable" and in this most attenuated sense "understandable" or "human" is trivial—it follows tautologically from the existence of the subject. And if the explanation of Hitler's behavior consisted in experiencing his hatreds and ambitions, then he would remain inexplicable for most people. There is, of course, an explanation for Hitler's behavior; it consists in causal analyses of abnormal psychology, in which identification with the subject and so "understanding" of the explanatory concepts has diminished to the vanishing point. On the other hand, an unrepentant Nazi could give the same causal analysis but find the explanation perfectly understandable. Understandability, or the lack of it, thus, is not itself a part of the explanation of Hitler's behavior, does not tell us anything more about *him;* but it does express important information about the personality of the *explainer.*

Finally, it is not the case that external physical and social environmental factors are useless in psychological explanations, that the factors must always be "psychological" or "internalized." It is true that the psychologist usually explains his subject's behavior by personality factors—not necessarily, however, as we have seen, by understandable ones. If this were the only explanatory function of a psychologist, however, it would leave completely inexplicable those chapters in every serious study of personality which concern the all-important early "formative years" of the subject. The point of such chapters is to show the part that social and physical environmental factors play in producing those personality factors which, in turn, explain behavior. Personality, as well as behavior, requires explanation and in this explanation environmental factors, both social and physical, play an important role.

The psychologist's task of explaining how personality

characteristics came about is not confined to the youthful years, for every year is formative for those that follow. The psychologist is constantly trying to explain the continuous changes, large and small, which occur in the life of the subject. To neglect this task of explaining personality development is to produce a Theophrastian character, not to unfold a life with its mercurial flights, its shades and lights. The nineteenth century emphasis on processes, changes, and evolution has left its mark on the psychology of personality as on everything else.

## FOUR

# Psychoanalytic Propositions

THE RELATIONS between psychoanalysis and philosophy are complex indeed and much discussed. On the one hand, philosophers of science have been busily analyzing the logical structure of psychoanalytic concepts and propositions, and they have generally not been too happy with the result.[1]* Their criticisms are of two sorts mainly. (1) Many psychoanalytic propositions are meaningless—or, at any rate, pointless—because they are in principle untestable. Moreover, many others, even though meaningful and testable, cannot be accepted as confirmed since they do not yield any significant predictions. (2) The concepts of Freud's metapsychology, like Eros, Thanatos, Id, Ego, and Superego, and the hypotheses using them are fantastically vague, but even worse they are metaphysically queer. The

* For the notes to Chapter Four see pages 136-38.

very notion of unconscious motives as existing entities which *cause* slips of tongue, dream contents, *et al.,* seems ontologically odd to the point of being meaningless.

On the other hand, some philosophers accept psycho-analysis more or less *in toto* and bend it to philosophical purposes. Several have used it to explain the obsessive com-mitments of metaphysicians to "philosophical" statements which are allegedly meaningless[2] while others have used it for varying purposes in moral philosophy, either claim-ing that it establishes the traditional determinism position or that it reinforces the common-sense notion of self-deter-minism.[3] I shall examine the philosophical critiques of psychoanalysis in the present chapter and the philosophical implications of psychoanalysis for moral philosophy in the next.

## A. ARE PSYCHOANALYTIC PROPOSITIONS UNCONFIRMABLE?

I shall examine first the allegation that psychoanalytic propositions are unconfirmable and hence scientifically meaningless—or at least pointless—and second, the con-tention that they are unconfirmed as a matter of fact. I shall finish by asking what sense the metapsychological notion of unconscious motivation, as a *vera causa,* might make.

If my watch runs slow and I explain it by saying a little blue devil gets his tail caught in the works, I must deduce some consequence and test it if this hypothesis is to be scientifically respectable. If I explain to someone who proposes unscrewing the back of the case and extricating the little devil that he can't because the little fellow is invisible, and moreover he is odorless, etc., too, then I protect my hypothesis from falsification by making it compatible with any state of affairs. Many philosophers of science have made precisely this claim about the nature of psychoanalytic propositions. They are framed and held in such a way that no evidence can count against them. Thus immune from falsification or disconfirmation they are also immune—although their proponents do not see it—from verification or confirmation. One writer cites Freud's concept of *archaic heritage* as a good example of this point.[4] Freud thought that dream analysis reveals "ideational contents" in the dreamer's unconscious which he could not have learned either from childhood or adult experience. Freud concluded that "we are obliged to regard it as part of the *archaic heritage* which a child brings with him into the world, before any experience of his own, as a result of the experiences of his ancestors."[5] But Freud's notion, of course, runs into headlong conflict with modern genetics; acquired characteristics cannot be inherited. But does the difficulty disconfirm the hypothesis for Freud? Not at all; he keeps the concept because "I cannot picture biological development proceeding without taking this factor into account." Thus this hypothesis is irrefutable and hence meaningless, or at least pointless. To be sure, most contemporary analysts do not accept this concept, but what then? If this concept of Freud's can be rejected and his others retained, *why could not this independence of theoretical notions be demonstrated to Freud himself?* Primarily because the concepts and hypotheses of psychoanalysis are so vague that it is not clear what is dependent on what, and what independent of what.

The answer to this criticism has several parts, but it is not very complex even so. First, psychoanalytic propositions are not all of the same logical type. So even if one type can be shown to be immune from disconfirmation and thus scientifically meaningless it does not follow that the other types also are. (Unhappily this implication is often present in the critic's argument.) Consider the following different types of psychoanalytic concepts[6]: (1) Eros and Thanatos; (2) psychosexual development, Oedipus complex; (3) fixation, trauma, etc.; and (4) Id, Ego, and Superego. The items in (2) are genetic concepts of development; the items in (3) are internal qualitative relations of these developments and processes to the demands of the environment; and the items of (4) are theoretical concepts —what I shall call intervening variables—which relate the concepts of (2) and (3). These are the inter-connected concepts of Freudian theory. The items of (1), Freud's instinct theory, to which the concept of archaic heritage belongs, are irrelevant to this body of imperfectly but decently related theoretical concepts. Thus, the critic's demolition of the concept of archaic heritage leaves the core of psychoanalytic teachings untouched. Second, to the question why the independence of (2), (3), and (4) from (1) could not be demonstrated to Freud, the answer is this: he was too close to his own theory and had more than rational attachment to all of his ideas, just as most of us do. One has no more right to assume that Freud could not see this independence because (1), (2), (3), and (4) are vague and blur together than he does to assume that Darwin could not see the irrelevance and untestability of his pangenesis theory because the concepts of natural selection and pangenesis are vague and blur together. Darwin's case is rather like Freud's in the sense we are insisting upon. Like Freud, Darwin was too close to his own work and more than rationally attached to his ideas to see the irrelevance of the concept of pangenesis. The existence of scientific societies and public forums attest to this universal fact of an individual's more than rational attachment to his ideas. It is gratuitous to ground one scientist's lack of insight on the vagueness of his own hypotheses when this lack would be explained in quite another way in other cases.

Another writer attacks one of the genetic concepts, claiming that it, too, and others like it, are in principle not testable and hence are scientifically meaningless. (Sometimes it is unclear whether critics are saying that analytic propositions are scientifically meaningless or simply pointless because of their alleged untestability.) Under what conditions, this writer asks,[7] is the psychoanalyst ready to admit that a child does not have an Oedipus complex? What kind of evidence is he prepared to accept to falsify the hypothesis that a specific child has an Oedipus complex?

Psychoanalysts have replied in the following vein. Unfortunately philosophers of science do not know much about psychoanalysis or they would distinguish between a fact of observation, the Oedipal phase, and a theoretical term, the Oedipus complex.[8] Then they give criteria which would falsify the claim that a child goes through an Oedipal phase. The criteria are complex but include this sort of thing[9]: if a little boy failed to express tender or romantic fantasies regarding his mother, if he failed to exhibit his penis, etc., if he were emotionally impulsive, if he had little identification with the standards of his human environment, and if he had little concern about others, then truly we could say he failed to go through an Oedipal phase. And there is a host of other criteria which could be appealed to for a decision. Philosophers of science counter this answer in the following way.[10] Is any one of these criteria *sufficient* to say that the Oedipal phase of development has not been reached? Or is each one *necessary* and the whole group together *sufficient?* But in this case the reference to a "host of other criteria" makes one wonder if there is such a finite list of necessary criteria. But this reply will not do. The psychoanalyst does not consider any one of the criteria as either necessary or sufficient, and he would consider the occurrence of all of them as staggeringly sufficient! The true situation, he believes, is this: a child may not, and usually will not, have *all* of the specified characteristics, but he must have *some* of them; and the more he has, and the more continuously and intensely they manifest themselves, the stronger the evidence becomes for saying he is or is not in an Oedipal phase.

To this sort of defense, the following further criticism has been addressed: To be sure, terms like 'Oedipus complex' do mean something, but the semantical rules governing their use are so complicated and so complex that only a skilled and highly experienced psychoanalyst can apply them. So it follows that only an expert "really understands" psychoanalytic theory. "But then it is easy to see why a philosopher might be suspicious, might wonder, in view of these labyrinthine rules [known only to the expert], whether the psychoanalyst is really ever *using the theory,* and not, rather, *simply* relying on intuition."[11] The proper answer to this criticism is straightforward: (1) It requires considerable training, responsibility, and experience to apply correctly a term in any field which is both a science and an art, or skill; (2) in all such fields— medicine, engineering, testing—it takes intuition, or a "feel" for the field, as well; (3) in all such fields only an expert can really understand the theory; (4) but it does not follow from any of this that such an expert in whatever field is not relying on whatever theory he has. He may not be, to be sure, but the criticism we have been examining does not establish it.

This reply can be amplified and the source of the critic's

error exposed if we consider for a moment the nature of early experimental psychology, specifically Wundtian structural psychology.[12] Wundtian psychology depended upon introspective analysis under an analytic set, in contrast to the phenomenological set, say, of Brentano's act psychology. The introspective analysis of classical psychology required considerable training, responsibility, and experience on the part of a psychologist if he were to engage in it successfully. One, indeed, had to have a "feel" for it —gained only after much practice. Moreover, only "experts" in the use of introspective techniques clearly understood all their aspects and nuances. But it does not follow from any of this that such an expert did not know what he was doing or *that someone else who would go through all the prerequisites of training, practice, etc., would not get the same results.* In fact, structural psychologists on most issues had a high degree of agreement.

To be sure, one might argue against the conclusion in the following way. Classical psychology foundered on the image-thought controversy, a controversy over an untestable concept. May we not expect psychoanalysis to founder for the same reason? A closer look at historical facts suggests that this reply will not do. Classical psychologists wondered if "thought contents" always occur within "mental images." Some of them, on introspective analysis, always discovered a mental image present and operative in their thought processes; others did not. The latter, then, insisted that some thought, at any rate, is imageless.[13] The

75

former, however, replied, not too graciously, that an image is always there if one is skillful enough in introspective analysis to discover it! Psychology, it seemed, had come upon evil times; the results achieved seemed to depend upon who did the analyzing. Now, of course, one or several such untestable notions, whether in classical psychology or psychoanalysis, would be neither sufficient reason for dismissing a science nor an adequate explanation of its demise if it did disappear. In fact, the demise of classical psychology was not caused by any untestable concepts or techniques; it died because research interest shifted from a desire to compile syndromatic-like inventories of consciousness to a desire to discover process-like explanations of behavior. Psychoanalysis, thus, couldn't fade away—desirably or not—on the same grounds classical psychology did, because it *is* a process-like series of explanations, and the only one we have, in the psychology of personality.

In addition to attacking the notion of Oedipus complex as untestable, philosophers have criticized many other genetic, structural, and theoretical concepts of psychoanalysis on the same ground (although one psychoanalyst points out in an *ad hominem* sort of way that it is no accident that philosophers are preoccupied with the Oedipus concept![14]). Counter-wish-fulfillment dreams, resistance to the analyst's interpretation, and unconscious hostility are just a few of the concepts which have come under fire. Philosophers have argued that all of them are immune to disconfirmation. Freud says all dreams are wish fulfillments. If a patient has a dream unconnected with any wish, does this count as disconfirmation? Not necessarily, the analyst replies, because the dream may fulfill the wish to produce a dream which does not fulfill a wish.[15] If a patient agrees with his analyst's interpretation, this response is taken as confirming its truth; but if he disagrees with the interpretation, this response is taken as a resistance to the true interpretation for unconscious causes.[16] Or, let us consider in detail the case of 'unconscious hostility.' (Everything said in this context holds for all three concepts and many more.) Suppose an analyst says a patient has an unconscious hostility toward his father.[17] What sort of findings would falsify this hypothesis? Supposedly if we observe that the patient acts with affection and solicitude toward his father. The analyst might deny that this evidence falsified his hypothesis, for the solicitude may be excessive and thus fit into the analytic hypothesis. Yet he is not, after all, protecting his hypothesis from disconfirmation altogether. If the solicitude is moderate and not excessive *this* fact would constitute genuine counter-evidence. Moreover, one might argue, this criticism is oversimplified since the hypothesis is only confirmed or disconfirmed by referring to a large range of facts. The hypothesis can be shown to be acceptable or not, only by referring to this total evidence. Certainly if a person, for example, does not tend to suppress and repress anger, never has dreams in which violence is directed at his father, never makes slips of the tongue which suggest abuse of his father, never "accidentally" breaks his father's belongings, etc., then the hypothesis of unconscious hostility toward his father is rejected. On the other hand, ". . . if there are a fairly large number of affirmative answers, then the hypothesis tends to be highly confirmed."[18]

What troubles some people in this sort of answer is this: to be sure, there are a number of facts relevant to the unconscious hostility hypothesis, and they are interrelated by analytic hypotheses, but can any of them be *predicted?* If X has dreams in which violence occurs toward an object X associates with his father, if X makes a *faux pas* which is associated with abuse of his father, and if X "accidentally" breaks his father's possessions, can we predict, say, that X will generally avoid the expression of conscious anger and will not feel conscious anger in situations which would ordinarily arouse it? Or from all the rest of the relevant facts can we predict X will "accidentally" break his father's possessions? In short, can we find any reliable response-response law which allows us to predict one behavioral response from another or a behavioral response from some childhood experience? Some writers would answer all of these questions negatively and thus condemn psychoanalysis as hopelessly vague and untestable and, hence, meaningless or pointless. Psychoanalysts "explain" after the fact by interpreting analytic factors in a way which yields the observed result, but they cannot use these factors in a precise way to predict the result. Since the psychoanalyst thus always plays the role of Epimetheus his hypotheses are genuinely untestable and of doubtful worth. However, it does not follow that if a hypothesis cannot predict it is thereby not testable and, in fact, not a warrantable knowledge claim. Many sociological explanations, most historical and biographical ones, and all natural selection explanations in biology are of this *post facto* sort. A person could not possibly have predicted, say, George W. Curtis' bolting the Republican party in 1880. It is true, he hated the spoils system and Blaine stood for it, but, after all, Curtis was a staunch Republican and wasn't he a member of the nominating convention and thus bound to accept its choice? The situation is complex; many factors enter in. Which is strongest; how do they relate to each other? These questions could not be answered until the event had occurred. Then we know his contempt for the spoils system is the strongest motivation in his political decisions. Yet certainly his contempt for the spoils system *explains* why he bolted the Republican party even though one could not have *predicted* he would act in this way. Simply because a hypothesis or explanation could not have functioned as a prediction it does not follow that it is "untestable" or even that it is not a good warrantable knowledge claim. Indeed, in this historical case it is. But why cannot psychoanalytical propositions, too, be explanatory, and thus perfectly meaningful and even true, even though not predictive? Perhaps they are not meaningful and true but nothing in the present criticism tends in the slightest to establish this point, and without this point the criticism collapses. To be sure, if a series of propositions claiming to be scientific cannot predict anything they are certainly robbed of one of the best ways of being tested and perhaps confirmed, but they are not robbed thereby of meaningfulness and even confirmation. Or if they are, no one has shown why. Least of all in the present context. The whole point is simply taken for granted. Finally, this criticism assumes that psychoanalytic propositions are not predictive, but this assumption is far from obvious. Analysts think they predict a great deal. This point, however, takes us into the next section. And we are ready to proceed to it since none of the claims that psychoanalysis is in principle unconfirmable seems to be defensible.

### B. ARE PSYCHOANALYTIC PROPOSITIONS UNCONFIRMED?

Most philosophers of science agree that psychoanalytical propositions are not confirmed. The claim here is this: while the propositions are testable and have some empirical meaning, we cannot tell whether or not what they assert is true. They simply have not been confirmed. I shall examine the major evidence for this conclusion in some detail and see what can be said against it.

The psychoanalytic interview is the method by which analysts arrive at their hypotheses and *by which they test them also.* In the interview, the analyst tries to discover the unfulfilled but repressed "wish" of early childhood, usually sexual in nature, which is causally effective, on the level of the unconscious, in producing neurotic conflict. The analyst tries to discover the nature of the wish and the neurotic conflict by interpreting the "latent meaning" of the patient's free associations, slips of tongue, and dream contents. Consequently, as Nagel says,[19] the crucial question is this: how do we confirm or validate such interpretations? Each "interpretation," one might say, is an analytical hypothesis; but the question is still this, how is it established as valid? Psychoanalysts, according to their philosophical critics,[20] would accept an interpretation as correct if it (1) is compatible with all things disclosed by the patient in the interview; (2) predicts specific consequences; (3) is an instance of a general law; and (4) is accepted by the patient as a true interpretation and has therapeutic consequences for him. However, the critics continue, analytical interpretations by and large are not confirmed: either a criterion is inadequate or else the interpretations fail to meet the criteria. (1) is an inadequate criterion. Simply because an interpretation is *compatible* with the facts does not make it a true explanation of them. The Ptolemaic hypothesis in a way was compatible with the facts but it turned out to be false even so. Moreover, it is a notorious fact that analysts themselves can give plausible alternative interpretations which are compatible with the same facts; but which, then, is the true one?

(2), (3), and (4) are adequate criteria but analytical interpretations do not really meet them in a significant way.

(2) What sort of predictions can the analyst make from his interpretation? Various reactions of the patient, apparently. The analyst, e.g., predicts the acceptance of an interpretation given and of sudden insight combined with the production of confirmatory details, such as the subject's recall of past experiences which he had been previously unable to remember, or substitute reactions of a wide variety. However, the critics say, this answer will not do. After all, the interpretation *itself* does not predict its own acceptance by the subject or an "insight" on his part. And it is difficult to see how the *acceptance* of an interpretation could ever be significant confirming evidence when it is a notorious fact that people often accept things for the wrong reasons. Moreover, the acceptance of an interpretation could not count as confirming evidence unless there is some information about negative cases. We need to know, after all, the percentage of cases in which similar subjects reject similar interpretations of their behavior, or the number of cases in which similar subjects do not have their behavior "illuminated" by such interpretations. Moreover, the 'recall of confirmatory details' is not without difficulty. It may well be that recall occurred simply from the overall prodding of the subject's memory during the interview rather than from the specific content of the analyst's interpretation. Furthermore, how do we know the object of recall—say a traumatic experience—genuinely occurred in the way remembered? When an adult recalls childhood events, he may well erroneously color

them in terms of his later experience, including that of the psychoanalytic interview itself.[21]

Finally, the analyst often has difficulty in making any objective prediction at all from his interpretations because he disturbs the interview situation by his own method of investigation. While the analyst is supposedly a passive hearer of his subject's "free-associations," as a matter of fact he often directs their course.[22] The point can be made ironically by saying a patient seems to dream in the dialect of whatever psychoanalyst happens to be treating him![23]

According to (3) an interpretation is confirmed if it is an instance of a general law. The analyst believes that one can distinguish various types of neurotic personality and that each type is in fact related to a fairly distinct kind of childhood traumatic experience. Thus, when the analyst discovers by means of the interview to which type his patient belongs, his interpretation is supported by an appeal to the corresponding law.[24] But, the argument goes, there is something queer about these alleged psychoanalytic laws. First, it is unclear whether a regularity holds between neurotic symptoms and what actually happened to a patient in childhood, or between the symptoms and what the patient *says* happened to him in childhood. The second kind of regularity, of course, would be utterly unreliable itself and thus would not lend evidential value to any specific interpretation. But the first kind of regularity is not acceptable either unless there is something known again about negative cases. As Nagel points out, it may well be the case that children with such-and-such traumatic experience develop into certain kinds of neurotic adults. But such evidence is valueless unless it can also be established that *normal* adults have not undergone the same sort of childhood experiences. "In short, data must be analysed so as to make possible comparisons on the basis of some *control* group, if they are to constitute cogent evidence for a causal inference."[25]

According to (4), an interpretation is confirmed if it is accepted by the patient and has a therapeutic effect on him. Or better, there is some sort of confirmation bestowed on analytic interpretations in general if they *tend* usually to have therapeutic effects. To be sure, therapeutic success is not *identical* with confirmation of analytic theory but it certainly is *a part of* the confirming procedure. But, the criticism goes, even successful therapy will not help confirm analytical propositions. Granted that analysis is followed by therapeutic success, it does not follow that this success was caused by analysis. It might have been the result of suggestion, or simply the result of talking out a problem with a sympathetic listener.[26] Moreover, success often occurs without psychoanalytic techniques. General practitioners apparently have the same ratio of successful therapy as analysts do.

The upshot of this discussion is this: granted that the analyst's interpretations are *confirmable*—that is, they have some empirical content, however vague—nevertheless these interpretations, since they do not successfully meet the analyst's own four criteria of confirmation, must be taken as *not confirmed.*

I am not quite convinced by this critique of psychoanalysis and will suggest in some detail what I take to be an adequate reply to it. (1) No analyst would ever dream of saying that the compatibility of his theory with clinical facts is a sufficient validation of them; this condition, of course, is simply an obvious necessary one. But the analyst believes—and I think rightly so—that this necessary condition is only met by analytical theory and thus, whether or not it yields detailed predictions, analytical theory has a good degree of antecedent probability clinging to it. True, Copernican theory was not verified simply because it was compatible with all the facts; the Ptolemaic theory was also, but it turned out to be false. The important point is this: in this case there are significant alternatives while psychoanalytic theory is the *only* hypothesis that knits together widely divergent facts about personality development and neurotic behavior. This fact makes the analyst believe that the compatability of his theory with the facts gives his theory an antecedent probability; but he would not dream of claiming this compatability alone sufficed to establish the theory. Analysts themselves, it is true, often give plausible alternative interpretations of the same clinical facts, but what does this prove? It proves that they disagree about what analytic hypotheses to apply to a specific case for explanatory purposes; it does not show disagreement over the basic hypotheses. This same sort of disagreement occurs in any "geophysical" type science where laws discovered under artificially controlled conditions are used to explain some concrete, unrepeatable course of events.[27] The conflicting interpretations of historical, geological, meteorological, archaeological, and anthropological data are notorious, yet order gradually emerges from the chaos. And certainly no one would think of using the simple fact of conflicting interpretations of specific data to throw doubt on the basic principles—often quite exact—used in these intellectual enterprises. So why should the fact of conflicting interpretations throw complete doubt on analytic principles? To be sure, analysts of different "schools" hold *different basic hypotheses,* although they accept many in common too, far more, in fact, than non-analysts would ever suspect from reading philosophical treatises on psychoanalysis. The disagreement usually occurs on the level of theoretical terms and the ones which are held in common are generally genetic and structural hypotheses. Such hypotheses as these, then, would still retain their antecedent probability. (Moreover, one must not accept every *prima facie* conflict as a genuine one, and one must not accept every conflict as a significant one either. Some people still believe the earth is flat but this conflict does not upset geographers! The same can be said for the conflicts generated by "fringe" psychoanalysts—the literary, philosophical, and amateur dabblers in analytic theories. Their activity does not upset the working analyst.)

(2) One must be very careful in saying what it is the analyst thinks he *predicts*. The analyst would readily agree that he does not predict as part of an analytical interpretation the patient's acceptance of it. Indeed, in some cases the interpretation, even though probably correct, is resisted by the patient. Then the analyst has the job of explaining this resistance. (Note well that the analyst does not explain every rejection of an interpretation in terms of the subject's resistance. To do so would indeed render such an interpretation untestable. Whether or not the analyst says the patient is resisting depends on the way the patient rejects the interpretation—out of hand and with considerable force or quietly and after consideration.[28]) But even though the acceptance of an interpretation is not predicted and often indeed is not accepted, does not the fact of acceptance offer support of some kind when it does occur? I think it does but only if the acceptance of the interpretation leads to uncovering forgotten events of childhood—for the existence of which there is some antecedent likelihood (knowledge of parental characteristics, environment, etc.), objective corroboration (documents, other people's memories, etc.), or lawful corroboration (exemplifying one of the genetic laws connecting a neurotic syndrome with specific childhood experiences). This sort of corroborating evidence, not really prediction in any sense at all, occurs in abundance in the clinical records. When it does not occur, then clearly the "memory" of a childhood experience does not count as confirming evidence for

the interpretation. (Certainly the analyst is fully aware of the treachery of his patient's "memory" in more ways than one! Freud saw more clearly than philosophical critics that some patients could not distinguish their fantasies from what actually happened.[29] Or through transference the patient's unconscious may submissively corroborate, through fantasies, dreams, and slips of tongue, a wrong interpretation. Or he may defiantly corroborate an interpretation *because* it is wrong! Obviously no analyst accepts such "memories" following the acceptance of an interpretation as confirming evidence—which, of course, is just another way of saying he does not take a remembered incident as confirming evidence unless it is corroborated.)

Furthermore the point about negative cases breaks down since comparable patients may well react differently to the same interpretation—some accepting and some resisting it. Then the analyst's job is to explain the resistance. (Certainly "comparable" cases cannot mean "identical cases." No analyst ever expects two patients to have identical syndromes and past experience! But if 'comparable' does not mean 'identical,' then two comparable patients may well respond quite differently to an interpretation, one accepting and one resisting it.)

Finally, it is true that the analyst *does* disturb the phenomenon under investigation but he is utterly aware of this as a part of his own theory. He has numerous corrective devices, including analytical knowledge of himself, and these devices have succeeded even in revealing observational error in other, more experimental branches of psychology.[30] Moreover, that some objectivity of prediction *is* as a matter of fact possible is revealed by the fact that a supervising analyst makes innumerable correct predictions about the development of a case and the appearance of certain specific material simply by using the record of a patient whom he has not even seen![31]

I have emphasized that the acceptance of an interpretation while it may be, under certain conditions, confirming evidence is not *predicted* by the analyst. What sort of thing, then, does he predict, if anything, and how do these predictions generally turn out? Do they tend to confirm or disconfirm analytical hypotheses?

Analysts using their genetic and structural hypotheses constantly predict in the following way. When they find some trait exhibited they can predict numerous different manifestations of it as well as closely allied traits and their resultant behavior. They also postdict the existence of certain childhood experiences associated with this syndrome of traits. Consider the following example cited by Jacob Arlow.[32] To the question "How long have you been married?" one patient replied, "Sixteen months, three weeks." From the overly precise nature of the response, Arlow assumed the existence of obsessional and compulsive traits. From this hypothesis he "predicted" the existence of a cluster of mental traits all of which, he discovered, did exist: the patient had a passion for accumulating money and keeping minutely detailed financial records; he was overly neat about his clothes, tidy in his habits; orderly, rigorously punctual, careful in meeting obligations, etc. Moreover, Arlow related this syndrome to a specific type of childhood experience in bowel training and interest in excrement, and again this "prediction" (postdiction) was verified. Such predictions, he concludes, occur hundreds of times in clinical cases—indeed they occur constantly —and hence cannot be simply the result of guesswork or intuition. Moreover, analysts constantly predict the kind of dream a patient is going to have, the kind of feelings he will manifest under specified conditions, and the kind of material he will produce,[33] and these predictions frequently hold true in fact.

Needless to say, there have been several criticisms of the significance and reliability of these psychoanalytical predictions. The negative case argument again: Even though these predictions are frequently true they do not significantly confirm an interpretation unless we know the frequency with which such predictions are incorrect.[34] But again this criticism will not do. Certainly no one would deny that these predictions often break down and this disconfirms the interpretation; hence the analyst has to *change* his interpretation. But if this is so, then it also follows that correct predictions tend to *confirm* a given interpretation.

Another criticism is this: analytical predictions are never precise, only approximative and often vague; thus they do not count much in the way of confirmation. The analyst may predict either overtly aggressive behavior or overly concerned behavior but cannot predict which specific one it will be. He may predict the form of a dream but not the content; he may predict types of behavior associated with traits but not specific acts, etc. Several replies to this criticism are possible. First, in some cases the predictions are, in fact, quite precise; these occur in the cases of uninformed children, naïve psychotics, and subjects under hypnosis. But it is true that in other cases the predictions may be only approximative and not at all precise. What then? One might say simply, psychoanalysis is only a protoscience; when its hypotheses are made more precise, its predictions will become more precise.[35] However this reply, while acceptable in a way, does not go to the heart of the matter. The best reason, I believe, for explaining why specific predictions are not always possible in ordinary neurotic cases is that learning and reasoning processes subsequent to childhood experiences require modification of the analytic hypotheses in ways not yet determined. Thus we need not simply greater precision of *analytic* hypotheses but also greater precision of learning hypotheses and greater precision in stating the ways in which they are both involved in interrelated ways in the explanation of ordinary neurotic cases. When we achieve this knowledge, then we will achieve more precise and not only approximative predictions in such cases. But the final point is this: although we cannot predict precisely the concrete course of a neurotic's life because we do not know how childhood and later experience mingle together to produce such a result, nevertheless it does not follow that our approximative and imprecise predictions fail to bestow *any* confirmation on analytic interpretations. Certainly if the approximative predictions turned out consistently to be wrong, this fact would go far to *disconfirm* the interpretations. Hence successful approximative predictions must tend to *confirm* them.

(3) Now we turn from criticisms of analytic interpretations to criticisms of the basic genetic and structural laws of psychoanalysis. From our discussion thus far it should be clear that these laws hold between neurotic symptoms and what actually happened to a patient in childhood, not between the symptoms and what the patient *says* happened to him in childhood. The laws themselves have been generalized from specific interview situations, and the analyst has of course constantly been on guard against accepting at face value what the patients report. As we have seen, patients often cannot distinguish betwen fantasy and fact and through identification erroneously recall incidents. Without antecedent probability and objective corroboration in the sense specified in the classic case histories, the laws themselves would never have come into being. Then, the laws themselves add their own confirming weight to subsequent cases where objective corroboration may be impossible to attain. To be sure, one would like always to get direct corroborating evidence—this would be the strongest sort of confirmation; but in the absence

of this, one still has *some* confirming evidence in the apparent applicability of a genetic or structural law.

But the negative cases point arises again for genetic and structural laws. We need a *control group* to see that there is not a significant percentage of men who undergo certain traumatic childhood experiences but nevertheless develop into reasonably normal adults before the fact that many men do have these experiences associated with later neurotic symptoms becomes a reliable law. At this point, the negative case argument must be taken seriously. It would be desirable, indeed, to have this information. Unhappily we are not likely to get it with the analytical movement isolated from the research advantages of academic institutions. It is, in fact, a good analytic question why most directors of such institutions resist incorporating any element of the movement in their offerings. Certainly as long as analysis occurs under the conditions it does— strictly as a medical enterprise with therapy as the immediate goal—we are not likely to get the statistical information about negative cases which is desired. But let us assume we have such information and that, as a matter of fact, there are numerous negative cases. *It still would not follow that childhood experiences were not the causes of the neurotic symptoms when they do occur.* Clearly experience subsequent to the early trauma effectively modifies results in some cases and not in others. The way such experience modifies the operation of analytic principles is the information we so desperately need to make the analytical principles *more* predictive and reliable. Again, this sort of knowledge is not likely to be forthcoming with the present status and restricted operation of analytical endeavor.

(4) Psychoanalysts themselves, as a matter of fact, generally depreciate the value of therapeutic success as confirming evidence for an interpretation.[36] Admittedly therapeutic success often occurs without analysis and hence its occurrence with analysis does not necessarily confirm an interpretation. But the analyst would point out, I believe, that according to analytical theory there is an *explanation* of his therapeutic success while this is not so with the success of the general practitioner. On the other hand, it is also true that therapeutic success sometimes does not result from using analytic techniques. Yet this fact need not be damaging since the analyst may have an acceptable explanation of a patient's resistance to a correct interpretation. But the gravest difficulty is this: even if success *does* follow analysis, how do we know it was the content of the interpretation that produced it? Perhaps it occurred simply from talking out a problem with a sympathetic friend, etc. To be sure, the analyst sometimes can explain under what conditions such "talking" has therapeutic effects and when not; but he realizes this reply is not a complete answer to the criticism. In any case, the analyst while making these various retorts for the purpose of clarification would agree that therapeutic success does not confirm his interpretations very much. But successful therapy is indirectly im-

portant. If he *never* had any success this would count heavily against his whole system of hypotheses!

The upshot of this long discussion is this: critics are not successful in showing that analytical hypotheses are simply *not confirmed.* True, they are not as well confirmed as some other scientific theories, but they do not lack confirmation altogether. They are, in my mind, sufficiently confirmed to make psychoanalysis a perfectly respectable proto-science.

### C. METAPSYCHOLOGY

Psychoanalysts use the concept of metapsychology to refer to the mental entities "beyond" conscious experience, namely, the unconscious motives, wishes, *et al.,* which are causally efficacious in producing neurotic symptoms. They sometimes use the concept more specifically to refer to "the most general assumptions of analysis on the most abstract level of theory."[37] Thus 'metapsychology' refers to the "substructures" of personality, the ego, id, and superego. In either of these senses philosophers of science have been quite critical of analytic metapsychology. The criticism usually takes two forms: (1) The notion of unconscious motives and wishes as *existing entities* which *cause* slips of tongue, dream contents, *et al.,* seems ontologically odd to the point of meaninglessness. The same is true for the alleged struggles among these entities, characterized by the concepts of ego, id, and superego. (2) Moreover, if these notions are interpreted in a way which makes sense of them, namely as definitional intervening variables, then they do not have any explanatory value. They are merely convenient abbreviations and nothing can be deduced with their help which cannot already be deduced from genetic and structural hypotheses. This criticism was suggested as long ago as the early part of the century when Pierre Janet referred to Freudian metapsychological notions as *une façon de parler*.

I shall examine these criticisms in detail, see what the analyst says by way of reply, and draw my own conclusions. I will agree with the criticism about ontological oddity and claim too that the concepts must be interpreted as intervening variables. But I shall argue that the critics misrepresent the concept of intervening variable and that when it is correctly understood, the analyst no longer need object to this interpretation.

(1) Philosophers of science have charged that unconscious motives are like "ghosts in a machine."[38] Freud's theoretical mental apparatus, conceived as unobservable entities with causal powers, simply reduplicates on an alleged psychic level the (unknown) somatic mechanisms which carry the "traces" of early traumatic experiences. "Accordingly, though psychoanalysis explicitly proclaims the view that human behavior has its roots in the biophysical and biochemical organization of the body, it actually postulates a veritable 'ghost in the machine' that does work which a biologically oriented psychology might

be expected to assign to the body."[39] Psychoanalytical metapsychology is thus anthropomorphic, the protestations of the analyst to the contrary notwithstanding.

Psychoanalysts might answer in the following way. Physicists infer the existence of unobservable atomic entities from observed events; analysts in the same legitimate way infer the existence of unconscious mental causes from observed neurotic behavior.[40] Only a restrictive positivist or operationist would deny the ontological significance of such concepts. After all, how does a physicist operate? He observes, e.g., that low frequencies of vibration of a string are connected with low pitches and higher frequencies with higher pitches. Is pitch a monotonically increasing function of frequency of vibration? No doubt it is. But soon the physicist reaches a point where the vibrations that presumably accompany a pitch are no longer observable. Then, "assuming that the causes of the higher pitches are sufficiently *analogous* to the causes of the lower pitches to warrant description in terms of the same concepts 'vibration' and 'frequency of vibration,' "[41] he infers the existence of unobservable vibrations. But, the analyst continues, we follow precisely the same logical procedure.

In psychoanalytic child therapy, for example, it is observed that a little boy exhibits just the sort of playing behavior that could be expected if he hated his father and sought to express this hatred through fiction, like painting a man and then splashing paint all over the picture. The boy fails to be aware of such

*97*

an evil emotion, so the analyst says that the emotion
exists in unconscious, repressed form.[42]

But this answer will not do, philosophers reply, since the
cases of unobserved vibrations and unobserved hates are
quite different. The concept of unobserved vibrations is
not ontologically queer since there is nothing about the
meaning of vibrations which requires them to be seen.
Thus in the phrases 'observable vibrations' and 'unobservable vibrations' the word vibration has the same meaning.
But the case of 'conscious hate' and 'unconscious hate' is
quite otherwise. To say "I hate X" implies, as part of its
meaning, that I am aware of, or conscious of, hating X.
Thus 'unconscious hate' is not a legitimate extension of
the meaning of 'hate' but is a self-contradictory extension
of the word. It is really discouraging to be told that you
really hate someone but are unaware of it. It is like being
told that you are thirsty but are not conscious of it. Anyone would insist that if he hated someone or were thirsty
he would be the first one to know about it, not the
analyst! True, the child may have had a traumatic childhood experience and this causes him, through a somatic
trace, to act in subtly aggressive ways; but it is fatuous to
say that he "really" hates his father although he does not
know it. It is true that one can be *mistaken* about what he
is introspectively aware of, but one cannot, in fact, be
introspectively mistaken in the sense that he thought he
did not hate his father but he was mistaken and really did.

We must distinguish between pure introspective awareness and such awarenesses plus a causal account of their
genesis. I may say, e.g., that I hate X because he is an
opportunist; but I may in fact be mistaken in my belief
and really hate X because he has got ahead of me in
salary and recognition. But in any case it is the causal
analysis of why I hate X that is mistaken. The chance of
being mistaken about hating X never arises since it is part
of the meaning of hating X, like it is part of the meaning
of being thirsty, that it is something we are aware of.

This sort of reply, it seems to me, effectively meets the
analyst's reply to the philosopher's criticism and establishes once and for all the ontological untenability of the
concept of unconscious entities which causally produce
neurotic symptoms. But the analyst—sometimes, I suspect, even seeing the justice of the philosopher's criticism
—still resists it. Why? The answer, I think, is this: the
analyst believes if he relinquishes the notion of unconscious entities with causal powers, then he can only
interpret 'unconscious motive,' *et al.,* and their "dynamic
relationships" (ego, id, and superego) as intervening variables, in contrast to hypothetical constructs—which he is
unwilling to do since he blindly accepts another of the
philosopher's criticisms, namely, that intervening variables
are merely convenient summaries or definitions and have
no explanatory value.[43] Since the analyst believes his concepts *do* have explanatory value he believes he must reject the intervening variable interpretation of them and

hold that they are hypothetical constructs. Hence he clings doggedly to his odd ontology. In the next section I shall claim that this interpretation of intervening variables is mistaken, that they do have explanatory value, and hence that the analyst need not desperately cling to his odd ontology in order to maintain the explanatory power of his metapsychological concepts.

(2) It is well known that the concept of intervening variable has long been used in psychology to refer to un-observable concepts "intervening" between observable stimulus and response events and explicitly defined by them.[44] In his learning theory, Hull, you recall, explicitly defines 'excitatory potential' as a function of 'habit strength' and 'drive'—$S^E R = f(S^H R \times D)$—and explicitly defines $S^H R$ and $D$ as functions of observable stimulus-response events. This terminology has spread throughout psychology, and 'intervening variable' has come to mean any non-model theoretical term in any area of psychology. Some analysts, in order to avoid the previous criticisms of ontological oddity, have wanted to interpret their own theoretical concepts like ego, id, and superego as intervening variables, and thus not referring to any entities with causal powers, but they have been deterred from doing so because they uncritically accepted the following interpretation of 'intervening variable.'

According to Meehl and MacCorquodale,[45] intervening variables are mere abbreviations and in principle eliminable. These terms, since they are only convenient summaries of thought and have no "excess meaning," are not helpful in deductively elaborating the hypotheses in which they occur. They distinguish from such variables what they call "hypothetical constructs." These "constructs" are not mere definitions but refer to actual entities in some model theory. Since they occur in a model theory they have the "excess meaning" which makes it possible to elaborate deductively the hypotheses in which they occur. However, the analyst need not be deterred from interpreting his own theoretical concepts as intervening variables instead of ontologically odd hypothetical constructs since this view of Meehl and MacCorquodale is clearly mistaken. Consider the notion of excess meaning. To be sure, the terms and hypotheses of any model theory must have "excess meaning" in the sense that it gives rise to deductive consequences other than the ones the theory was designed explicitly to explain. The kinetic theory of gases allows for the deductive development of consequences about gas behavior which were not anticipated by thermodynamic theory alone. But, of course, *the same can be said of any non-model theory, too.* Anything worthy of the name theory in science, in fact, has "excess meaning" in this sense. The essence of any non-model theory is twofold. First, fundamental laws describe the interaction of a limited number of variables in what is therefore called an elementary situation. Second, a composition rule, itself experimentally discovered, states how to form the laws of a complex situation in which many variables interact by conceptually decomposing it into elementary situations and reapplying a fundamental law to the parts. But intervening variables function in precisely the same way; they act as part of a non-model theory which predicts and explains behavior different from that on which they were based and thus have "excess meaning." Spence, as we have seen,[46] uses the concepts of cumulative strengthening of $S^HR$ (fundamental law of an elementary situation) and generalization (composition-like rule) to derive deductively certain transposition phenomena (which were not involved in the formulation of the laws). The derivation may not hold, as seems likely now, but this fact could not have been discovered unless the concept operated in a genuine theory with excess meaning. Moreover, Hull's concept of afferent neural interaction (despite its physiological sound) is again an intervening variable which has the status of a composition principle. The theoretical concepts of psychoanalysis too, conceived as intervening variables, can just as well have similar "excess meaning" in the sense of having explanatory power—at any rate, there is nothing in the notion of intervening variable that prevents them from having it. I am not claiming that psychoanalysis, in fact, does have fundamental laws and composition-like rules, but I am saying that it logically *can* have them while still interpreting ego, id, and superego as intervening variables. Indeed, the analyst may feel he does not have explanatory principles in these precise senses but still feel that his concepts genuinely have *some* explanatory value. This view, also, of course, is compatible with interpreting his theoretical concepts as intervening variables. The final conclusion, then, is this: if the analyst wishes to avoid odd ontological commitments by interpreting his theoretical concepts as intervening variables he is perfectly free to do so without thereby admitting that they have no explanatory function. I hope that the realization of this logical fact will convince more analysts to leave the dubious ground of "metaphysical science" and consolidate instead into a sensible whole their fascinating genetic and structural hypotheses with a scientific metapsychology.

# FIVE

# Psychoanalysis and Responsibility

I SHALL BEGIN with a rather lengthy statement of the traditional problem of determinism and moral responsibility in order to show clearly how psychoanalysis figures in its dialectical development. I shall argue, however, that psychoanalysis supports neither "determinism" nor "free-will," as different writers have urged; indeed I will contend that it is really irrelevant to this philosophical problem and that efforts to show its relevance tend to obscure the real import of psychoanalysis for moral philosophy. Finally I shall spend a good part of the chapter analysing what I take to be this real import.

## A. THE DETERMINISM ISSUE

The problem concerning determinism and moral responsibility arises in the following way. Modern science seems to provide a notion of cause, quite distinct from Aristotle's final cause, which implies that if something is caused then it could not be other than it is. If I have a genuine instance of a cause (that is, if I am not mistaken), then a certain effect *must* occur. It could not be otherwise, for if something else *could* occur then the cause is still unknown. If the concepts of cause and determinism applied only to physical objects there would be no trouble, but these concepts also apply to human behavior and here the perplexities begin to arise. If human behavior, too, is caused or determined, then *it* could not be other than it is. But moral judgments of behavior, on the other hand, are meaningful only if it *is* possible for behavior to be other than it is. If I say, "You ought not to beat your wife," I presume, if this judgment is to be sensible, that you could either beat or not beat her, that you chose the former course, and that I am morally condemning you for making the wrong choice. Apparently, then, science and moral philosophy come into headlong conflict. If human behavior is caused, then it could not be other than it is; if human behavior is morally judgeable, then it could have been other than it is. Hence, either human behavior is not caused, or else it is not morally responsible. Or, putting the point positively, either human behavior is caused, or it is morally responsible—but not both.

This traditional way of formulating the problem of determinism and moral responsibility is still accepted by many scientists and philosophers, although, as you may guess, it has serious flaws. Accepting this formulation, a person apparently has only two choices: he may either say that behavior is morally judgeable so not caused, in which case he is an "indeterminist," or he may say that behavior is caused so not morally judgeable, in which case he is a "determinist." Indeterminists do not in fact generally hold that all human behavior is uncaused; on the contrary, psychology, sociology, and all the other human sciences tell us a great deal about what causes personality traits, group behavior, and so on. Nevertheless, in choice situations there is, finally, a decision of will, freely made, for which the moral agent is responsible and, hence, judgeable.

However, there seems to be a difficulty with this claim. If the indeterminist strictly means that choices are not caused at all then he must admit that the agent who acted one way under certain conditions may subsequently act in an entirely different way under the same conditions, even though he himself has not changed at all. But this way out of the deterministic dilemma is no help, for it does not introduce moral responsibility but simply straightforward caprice. Moral responsibility demands the presence of something positive, not simply the absence of determinism.

*Psychoanalysis and Responsibility*

Determinism, on the other hand, seems equally as untenable as indeterminism. There are a number of reasons why this is so, but the simplest and most convincing is that determinism is self-destructive. If determinism were correct, "then our thoughts and the conclusions to which they lead would in every last detail be conditioned by factors which wholly antedated the thinking processes themselves. Evaluation or discrimination between better and worse, true and false, would be inexplicable and futile. Hence no rational defense of determinism would be possible. In short, if determinism is true, it is undemonstrable."[1]*

Since there is something artificial and untenable about both indeterminism and determinism, philosophers have come to suspect that the very formulation of the determinism issue which spawned them is confused. They have suggested that perhaps a further analysis of 'cause' and 'determinism' will dispel the whole problem with its strained alternatives. After all, behavior can be caused or determined in two radically different ways. Heredity and early environment are "external causes" over which we had no control but which nevertheless made us, in some sense, the way we are. To the extent that these factors control behavior—"by mechanisms behind the scenes"—a person indeed is not "free" and morally responsible. On the other hand, reason, imagination, and insight, along with a host of other subtle factors, are "internal causes" over which I have control and which quite obviously also

* For the notes to Chapter 5 see pages 138-43.

*107*

determine my behavior. To the extent that these factors control behavior, a person is indeed morally responsible. In fact, this notion of a reasonable being who can consider the consequences of his acts, unlike that of 'uncaused choice,' is the ordinary meaning of 'morally responsible.' Therefore, according to the present argument, while it is true that all behavior is caused, nevertheless some behavior is morally responsible, namely, that which is self-caused. This concept of self-cause can depend either on a complicated Kantian transcendental self or on a simple common-sense view that man is capable of acting on reasons rather than simply using them as rationalizations.

At this point in the dialectic of the determinism issue the cry has arisen that psychoanalysis shows that moral judgments are impossible or nonsense. According to this view, psychoanalysis annihilates the concept of self-cause, and thus this new way of salvaging moral responsibility comes to naught.[2] The psychoanalyst, after all, tells us that our behavior, including our so-called reasonable behavior, is really unconsciously determined and that conscious, reasonable life is merely a facade of rationalizations. "The unconscious is the master of every fate and the captain of every soul." However, it seems clear that this attempt to bolster determinism through psychoanalysis will not do. Psychoanalysts do not in fact usually claim that all *prima facie* reasonable behavior is unconsciously determined, for this view, of course, would deny that there are any objective or rational grounds for accepting the tenets of psychoanalysis itself—it would be self-destructive in the same way that traditional determinism is. The psychoanalyst's point is, rather, that much less behavior than anyone dreamed possible is free or responsible in the ordinary sense that it is consciously and reasonably shaped. However, this point is clearly irrelevant to the traditional determinism puzzle; for this puzzle simply disappears with the acceptance of the qualified statement, 'Most behavior is not free' or 'Very little behavior is free.' The puzzle only arises if all behavior is said to be determined in a way which implies it could not have been otherwise.

Some philosophers, on the other hand, have argued that psychoanalysis, far from annihilating the common-sense concept of self-determinism, actually provides the very techniques for deciding when and how much self-determinism or "freedom" a person has.[3] The analyst's techniques establish what behavior is obsessive, non-obsessive but unconscious, and rational—and, consequently, the argument goes, these techniques establish what behavior is nonresponsible and what responsible. And, after all, the point and frequent result of therapy is to produce freedom and responsibility where it did not exist before. More generally, some writers[4] argue that psychoanalysis, far from destroying the possibility of freedom, re-emphasizes the distinction between "reasons for action" and "causes of action" in its own employment of the "reason" or "motive" model of explanation rather than the efficient cause model. The analyst sometimes is misled by his hydraulic metaphors into thinking he has found efficient causes but only the physiologist with his palpable neurons can find the efficient causes of mental phenomena.

The common strain in all these views is that psycho-analysis reinforces or even establishes common-sense self-determinism and so salvages the notion of moral responsibility. This type of argument, however, misses the heart of the determinist's puzzle. Its irrelevance to the core of the puzzle is pointed up by imagining how a determinist would reply to it. He would say that he knows perfectly well there are common-sense tests which one uses to show a person could have done otherwise (by showing that he has the ability, displayed on other occasions, to do the alternate type of act and was under no duress to do the act he did) and scientific tests which one applies for distinguishing obsessive, non-obsessive but unconscious, and rational behavior; so that it makes sense both commonsensically and scientifically to make the distinction between free and unfree, responsible and nonresponsible acts; but nevertheless what he wants is proof that even in allegedly free acts we are not, without knowing it, being determined by neurotic or normal unconscious motivation beyond the range of our most careful tests to detect. This problem is the philosophical core of the determinist's position, since self-determinism, whether idealistic or commonsensical, plus the existentialist insight (namely, that in normal or non-neurotic behavior the point is not that man *is* responsible but that he *becomes* responsible as the price of maturity, of no longer being a child, and thus that he does *accept* responsibility for the consequences of his personality and character even though he had no control over their formation), easily avoids the original dilemma of the determinist. The determinist's real puzzle is the isomorph of a number of other philosophical puzzles. Even though there are accepted techniques for distinguishing veridical and illusory perception, how can I prove, or (Descartes's evil genius?) how can I be sure, that the allegedly veridical ones are not illusory or hallucinatory beyond the range of the accepted techniques—a crucial step in the dialectic of the issue over our knowledge of the external world. From this paradigm of philosophical puzzles, which in cludes science in its scope, psychoanalysis clearly cannot rescue us.

To be sure, one might argue that the issue which the determinist raises is spurious and the proof he demands nonsensical. He might try to show that the determinist's use of "free" in "For all we know we are really never free" is self-contradictory because the ordinary sense of "freedom," which he is apparently using (for otherwise the word is vacuous because he does not specify another meaning), is defined by the kind of thing which is evidence for the term's exemplification. Or one may cast his lot with common sense on other grounds, namely, that a property and predicate are "meaningful" over and above the tests of presence or applicability. In either case, however, the dialectic of determinism has eventuated in the dialectic of meaningfulness, which obviously antedates, logically, any empirical findings. Consequently, whether the issue the determinist raises is real or spurious, psychoanalysis has nothing to do with solving or dissolving it.

In this problem, psychology does not have philosophical results but philosophy has psychological results. When one realizes the true nature of the determinist's position (demand) his original perplexity is attenuated. What I have in mind is this. If one believes that the determinist's demand has not been parried successfully, he will admit, nevertheless, if he is honest with himself, that as a result of the dialectical drift he does not worry about the issue in the way that he did originally. He worried that the determinist had shown his ordinary views on freedom to be wrong, but it turns out simply that he has not proved they are right. But this ubiquitous problem—How can I be sure what I naïvely think to be true really is so?—is the paradigm of philosophical puzzles, and is not peculiar to a moral context, is not dependent on it for its formation. So the original perplexity and worry loses its force and urgency. A paradoxical way of saying the same thing is that a person worries less about determinism because he has to worry about the same problem everywhere. I think one could defend the view that therapeutic and casuistic positivists frequently confuse the attenuation of a philosophical problem with its dissolution and that the obvious fact that there is at least one philosophical problem that cannot be attenuated reflects the existence of the unannounced meaning criterion of the philosophical therapists and casuists.

## B. THE REAL IMPORT

There are numerous other ways in which psychoanalysis and morality get mixed together to the benefit of neither and the obscuration of the real import of the former for the latter; all that one can do is be alert to the danger and concentrate steadily on the real import, which is the view, long defended by most forensic psychiatrists, that neurotic behavior is nonresponsible. Some philosophers, along with the forensic psychiatrists, have defended this view; and the argument usually relied on is, roughly, the following: Neurotic behavior is nonresponsible because childhood neuroses cause adult neuroses, which, in turn, eventuate in criminal or queer behavior. But since a person has no control over the formation of his childhood neurosis, and no control over what follows inevitably from it, he cannot be held responsible for these consequences. The point of therapy, of course, is to make it possible for the neurotic to accept responsibility in the ordinary sense of the word; but *prior* to therapy, or where therapy has not occurred or is unsuccessful, the "malevolent" nature of the neurotic's unconscious makes him nonresponsible for his behavior. One must be careful, at this point, not to extend the claim of nonresponsibility to normal unconscious behavior because this extension brings in a host of additional issues and usually culminates in the old confusion of making the general determinist claim that one is nonresponsible because he had no control over the formation of his personality, to which claim the existentialist position is again applicable.

The juristic view of legal and moral responsibility, however, is far from hospitable to the psychiatrist's claim that neurotic behavior is nonresponsible; indeed the struggles in court between lawyer and psychiatrist even in the rare cases where the medical psychopathologist represents the court and not the plaintiff or defendant, have become notorious.

On the juristic view of the matter, a person is legally and presumably morally responsible if, or because, he is able, or has the capacity, "to tell the difference between right and wrong"; if, or because, he "knows the consequences, both legal and moral, of his act." This rule is the famous McNaghten Rule the jurist relies on, the legal definition of sanity and insanity; but it simply incorporates what is apparently obvious common sense. In criminal law this view is again reflected in the concept of *mens rea*. Jurists speak of the mental element in criminal liability (*mens rea*) and by this phrase they mean knowledge of consequences, foresight, intention, voluntariness, etc. One can disallow the presence of *mens rea*, or mitigate it, or simply defeat the allegation of responsibility, only if he can present defenses or exceptions like duress, provocation, infancy, or insanity. However, since the neurotic person meets the requirement of knowing consequences, etc., and is not under duress, or provoked, or insane, he cannot be judged otherwise by the court than as legally and morally responsible for his acts.

The McNaghten Rule, it should be noted at the outset, not only prevents the psychiatrist from making a case for the nonresponsibility of a neurotic individual but even makes it extremely difficult for him to establish the nonresponsibility of the psychotic. A person plans his own death; he murders another intending to get caught so he will be executed. The judge in the case, applying the McNaghten Rule, held the man clearly sane and responsible because he deliberately acted in terms of consequences![5] This consequence of the McNaghten Rule amounts to a *reductio ad absurdum* and clearly points up the psychological naïveté of the legalistic view; a naïveté which, as we shall see, is again reflected in the deterrence theory of punishment; but it remains to give direct reasons why this view is naïve, and to present counter-stimuli which may help carry the day over deep-seated fears and anxieties. The forensic psychiatrists, I believe, are more successful in these endeavors than philosophical interpreters of psychoanalysis because they do not rest content, the way the latter do, with establishing the nonresponsibility of neurotic behavior by using the previous argument about origins—although, to be sure, this argument is important. A number of remarks would be necessary for complete clarity but two fundamental ones must suffice for now.

1. The McNaghten type rule is psychologically unrealistic because it is possible to know the consequences of an act without having any feeling for them and thus without understanding them. The flattening or dulling of emotional tone, or its complete absence—"the failure to feel" —results from many severe psychopathological reactions, and it plays an important role in many different kinds of criminal personalities. Within these personality types, a person understands emotional life only in the way a blind man "understands" color; he may know things *about* it, what causes it, what effects it has, etc., but he does not *experience* it. Such a person is incapable of *feeling* the force and import of consequences; he is like a person in a dream state or under the influence of drugs. In short, his reason—in the sense of knowing what consequences will follow from certain acts—and his feeling tones have split apart or disintegrated, and psychological trouble is bound to start. Such a breakdown opens the door to aggression of all types. According to a noted forensic psychiatrist, "the considerable diminution or absence of emotion, or 'affect' as we say, is probably the most virulent phenomenon leading to the paralysis of moral judgment. . . ."[6]

Psychoanalysts have known and recognized this fact for a long time yet our legal system has no way of taking it into account. And the fact is so little known generally that the public completely mis-reads the nature of this sort of criminal. They assess his emotional indifference as moral indifference, callousness, incorrigibility, and depravity and thus they become prey to all sorts of feelings of counter-aggression and to an eventual vindictively motivated desire for retribution.[7] Who does not feel revulsion when a child's murderer asks for comic books to read in his cell because he is bored? But the crucial point, of course, is this: if such a criminal were capable of experiencing regret he would not have the diminution of affect that made his crime possible in the first place. Such a person is not a fit object of retribution because he is not responsible, and he is not responsible because he is incapable, through psychopathic causes, of adequate feeling tones for the consequences he "understood" would occur.

2. Rules of the McNaghten type are psychologically unrealistic and pernicious in their effects because (a) they depend on fragmentary criteria where understanding of the whole personality is needed and (b) they utilize formal, universally applicable criteria where individual analysis and insight is needed.

(a) In a case previously mentioned, a man murdered a youth because he wished to be apprehended and hanged. The judge in the case declared that since he knew the *consequences* of his act quite well, he knew the "nature and quality of the act," the usual terminology of McNaghten type rules, and was thus responsible for the act. He was hanged accordingly, before which, however, the prisoner happily expressed his appreciation! Cases like this one, some of which are more refined and accordingly less dramatic, more than formal analysis, make it abundantly clear that one cannot infer that another understands "the nature and quality of an act," where this means its moral import, because he manipulated it or used it in a utilitarian fashion, or because he reacted to it with any other isolated rational or emotional response. The only way to understand how a person construes "the nature and quality of an act" is in terms of the harmony of his total personality—particularly when it is the insane harmony of a pathological mind or the queer harmony of a neurotic one.

(b) Rules of the McNaghten type are, technically, non-vague; they either apply or do not apply to every individual; but the psychological facts are such that make this application wholly arbitrary and itself immoral. The analyst finds that each individual case is not simply different but unique; he needs to know the whole historical background of an individual case in order to "diagnose" psychosis, neurosis, etc., and whether and what therapy is applicable and might successfully rehabilitate. Psychiatry by its very nature cannot be formalized either as a clinical system or as a therapeutic method.

When a formalistic clinical attitude is assumed in psychiatry, the psychiatrist loses his usefulness as a healer; but strange as it may seem, he may gain in stature as a psychiatric expert. For if he feels that he can classify mental diseases with precision, and if he feels he can look upon the individual as the sum total of so many logical categories, and formal principles, he can fit himself and his opinions perfectly into the mold of the verbal metaphysics of certain aspects of the law.[8]

Such a formalistic psychiatrist, of which there are few, can, in short, do what the law demands of him in court, namely, apply rules of the McNaghten type. But for the rest of the psychiatrists this legal demand is untenable. This untenability arises, it is evident, because the psychiatrist is asked to determine the applicability of universal legal rules by psychological methods which not only do not accommodate these concepts but repudiate them.[9] The crucial point is that if law is to make judgments about responsibility which are themselves moral each case must be judged in terms of its specific circumstances, the statement of which the Qualified Forensic Psychiatrist is alone competent to make.[10]

Now we have come to the heart of the conflict between law and psychiatry. The law insists that the essence of a legal rule is its universal applicability and refuses, and no doubt will continue to refuse, to have its judgments of responsibility usurped by psychoanalysts even if their science were perfected more than it is. To make every case a special case, they point out, is legally impossible and would lead to legal nihilism. Better to gas or electrocute a neurotic here and there than to have the legal structure collapse. The psychiatrist, on the other hand, feels indignation over what he rightfully takes to be unjust executions. The only solution to this impasse, I strongly believe, is to take the psychiatrist out of court procedure entirely—

he neither applies McNaghten type rules nor gives technical testimony about the peculiarities of a given case in order to establish responsibility or its absence—abolish capital punishment, and allow the psychiatrist to work for the rehabilitation of neurotically motivated criminals during the period of their incarceration. It seems to me that only the abolition of capital punishment can resolve the conflict between law and psychiatric knowledge, and this resolution is the strongest and most completely unsentimental argument in favor of the abolition of capital punishment. In the incarceration period, moreover, the law must not simply "allow" psychiatrists to work at rehabilitation. The law must give status to the psychiatrist's role here and make a massive effort possible. The expense would be great, to be sure, but the expense of not doing it is far greater. Moreover, a first rate psychiatrist would be the first to admit that not all criminals can be rehabilitated because they are not all neurotically motivated. The professional criminal has an ethic all his own and is entirely beyond the pale of the analyst. The analyst's recognition of this fact should go a long way toward dispelling the hostility the jurist and penologist take to what they think is a sentimental and soft view, namely, that all criminals are neurotics and, poor things, could not help themselves.

## C. THEORIES OF PUNISHMENT

The present interpretation of psychiatry implies a rehabilitative "theory of punishment," the relation of which to the rival Kantian and utilitarian "theories" is usually far from clear. This traditional three-way classification, unfortunately, has more than one basis of division. If behavior is responsible, then Kantian and utilitarian theories are the significant alternatives (there is no rehabilitation to be achieved in non-neurotic behavior); but if behavior is nonresponsible, then rehabilitation and utilitarianism are the significant alternatives. Utilitarianism, unlike Kantian penology, is still a meaningful theory if behavior is nonresponsible because on this view punishment, and the pain it inflicts, is not intrinsically good but instrumentally good in preventing further more intense and overall greater pain. Punishment (preferably simple incarceration) achieves this end, the utilitarian believes, by protecting society and acting as an example that is effective in deterring not only the criminal himself from further criminal acts but also the potential criminal from acting out his wishes. Kantian and utilitarian theories are mutually exclusive theories of punishment if behavior is responsible. Protection and deterrence, for Kant, could never be legitimate reasons for punishing a person, but only desirable consequences of punishment. (One can, of course, try to show that both deontological and teleological justifications of punishment are exaggerations of different strands of common sense and that each in its own way is a "good reason" for punishment.) However, rehabilitation and utilitarianism are not mutually exclusive theories of punishment if behavior is nonresponsible; they are related in oblique ways, competitive in a sense but not mutually exclusive. For the person who believes that neurotic behavior is nonresponsible, the clarification of this oblique, and generally misunderstood, relationship is a most urgent need of penological theory.

The difficulty with the utilitarian example or deterrence view, the analyst feels, is not in principle, but simply that it does not do what it is supposed to do. Pickpockets plied their trade most avidly at executions, when all eyes were focused on the gallows, at a time when robbery itself was punishable by death![11] And comparisons among states which do and do not have capital punishment seem to indicate a lack of deterrence by harsh example (although there is sensible counter-evidence on this point).[12] This deterrence view is psychologically naïve because it does not take into account the neurotic roots of much crime, which renders rational deterrence irrelevant. And without the techniques of rehabilitation which do take these factors into account, straightforward punishment simply does not deter the criminal from repeating his behavior. "What the law . . . fails to see is that punishment alone inflicted from outside produces only a hostile response, an intensification of hatred, and consequently the diminution of those healthy, auto-punitive, restorative trends in man, which alone make man capable of inwardly accepting punishment and making salutary use of it."[13]

Rehabilitation and utilitarian social protection are in one sense obviously compatible. During rehabilitation the criminal is incarcerated and society is duly protected. However it follows that if the rehabilitation process appears successful the patient then has the *right* to be returned to society. Psychiatrists, however, meet great public indignation at either the idea or fact of the criminal's return. Analysts explain the vehement hostility of this objection in the following way. People identify themselves with the criminal's own impulses (who has not had them?) and are tempted to give way to the impulses. They become anxious and feel guilty, and are quieted by a sudden, unconscious denial of similarity with the criminal—and so react with great destructive hostility toward him. These causal analyses are usually justified but nevertheless one must not overlook the rational basis which underlies non-hysterical objections to returning the criminal to society—namely, a lack of confidence in the success and permanency of psychoanalytic therapy. Since psychiatry and psychoanalysis are not developed and certain sciences and since psychiatrists and analysts differ much among themselves on theoretical concepts, one must proceed cautiously, for the protection of society, in the return of rehabilitated criminals. One psychiatrist, in meeting the criticism of theoretic disagreement, writes that after all there is considerable disagreement in all areas of science, including the most rigorous—witness the disagreements of Einstein, Heisenberg, and DeBroglie—without impugning their reliability.[14] This type of defense, completely ignoring levels of disagreement, can only heighten the critic's suspicion that analysts are not always clear about what they are doing!

There is, finally, a regrettable tendency among certain

forensic psychiatrists to sentimentalize their antagonism to utilitarian views in a position they call "individualistic humanism." They condemn "legal utilitarianism" because it submerges the rights of the individual in a metaphysical entity, society, etc. A utilitarian, of course, is astonished at *this* sort of criticism because his notion of the greatest good is individualistic to the core—the largest amount of mutually compatible experienced goods. The psychiatrist's quarrel with utilitarian morality is a matter of detail, not principle.

# NOTES

## CHAPTER ONE
### Wholes and Parts

1. In W. D. Ellis, *A Source Book of Gestalt Psychology* (New York: The Humanities Press, 1950), p. 3.

2. *Ibid.*, p. 1.

3. *Ibid.*, p. 2.

4. *Ibid.*

5. Wolfgang Köhler, *The Place of Value in a World of Facts* (New York: Liveright, 1938), p. 205.

6. Cf. K. Grelling and P. Oppenheim, "Der Gestaltbegriff im Licht der neuen Logik," *Erkenntnis*, 7 (1938), pp. 211-24.

7. Ellis, *op. cit.*, p. 2.

8. *Ibid.*, p. 12.

9. *Ibid.*, pp. 71ff.

10. Köhler, *op. cit.*, pp. 194ff.

11. *Ibid.*, p. 201.

12. Ellis, *op. cit.*, p. 4.

13. *Ibid.*, p. 2.

14. Kurt Koffka, *Principles of Gestalt Psychology* (New York: Harcourt, Brace and Co., 1935), p. 57.

15. Wolfgang Köhler, *Dynamics in Psychology* (New York: Liveright, 1940), p. 55.

16. Köhler, *The Place of Value in a World of Facts,* p. 254.

17. Mr. Nicholas Rescher has questioned my use of "analytic" in this chapter. (Cf. his "Mr. Madden on Gestalt Theory," *Philosophy of Science, 20,* 1953.) I believe my use is entirely clear but nevertheless offer the following by way of answer to him:

Wertheimer and Köhler have both described the procedures of science and have in certain instances found them wanting. Wertheimer wrote that science characteristically attempts to "isolate the elements [of complexes], discover their laws, then reassemble them, . . ." and Köhler wrote that in " 'analytical' science . . . the properties of more complex extended facts are deduced from the properties of independent local elements." They claim, however, that certain areas of science cannot be adequately described in these analytical terms but must be described in Gestalt terms.

As an example of the "analytical science" to which they have reference I described the classical Newtonian problem of $n$ bodies, showing how a composition rule allows for the prediction of behavior of a complex configuration from the reapplication of the computation rule to the elements of a complex. This description constituted the analytical language of my chapter. In this language I tried to formulate certain Gestalt concepts—dynamic interaction, the whole is greater than the sum of its parts, etc.—and thus show that they occur already in "analytical physics" and are not, as the Gestalters believe, unique to what they call the non-analytical parts of physics. I hope this clarifies the use of "analytical" in this chapter, for without an understanding of it I do not see how any part of it would be clear.

My chapter is also "analytical" in a broader, less special sense. The designation of "analysis" or "analytical" in contemporary philosophical literature is usually 'clarification of meaning rather than ascertainment of truth or falsity.' Analysts, while they differ much in what they say and do, claim that the philosopher does not pass on the truth of common sense or scientific statements, but rather that he gives a more or less elaborate explication of such philosophical concepts as cause, substance, true, etc., and the sentences in which they occur. In philosophy of science the analyst clarifies such scientific concepts as variable, law, emergence, etc., and the statements in which they occur but himself makes no truth claim using these concepts. This analytical function of clarification rather than verification is the criterion which distinguishes the logician of science from the scientist. My chapter is analytical in this broad sense of "analysis" because I tried to clarify those Gestalt concepts and the statements using them which are relevant to scientific description and explanation by showing that they are already meaningful in the area of "analytical" physics.

Mr. Rescher writes that the "analytical" view is apparently taken as involving the denial of the Gestalt thesis that some perceptual properties of wholes are emergent relative to physical properties of parts and known psychological theories. However, this anti-Gestalt thesis is an assertion about psychological facts; it is a matter of truth or falsity which requires scientific ascertainment and so is beyond the pale of a logical analysis, such as mine, which clarifies systems of scientific sentences on whose truth it does not pass, let alone anticipate. To show that the meanings of specified Gestalt phrases can be rendered in a language which describes computation and composition rules which have been established is not to make any truth claims about where computation or composition rules will be found or to deny the breakdown of composition rules—emergence—in physics, psychology, or any area. The same things can be said about Rescher's statement that it could be claimed that the Gestalt thesis of emergence which he sketched is itself analytical. So we see that neither Mr. Rescher's statement of the Gestalt thesis nor its denial is analytical in the senses of "analysis" that are relevant to my chapter.

Considering Mr. Rescher's statement of the Gestalt thesis and its denial as truth claims in psychology, I have several brief comments to make. It seems pointless for psychologists to make either claim on *a priori* grounds, unless heuristically, when the answer depends upon scientific achievement or lack of it. However, the "analytical" view of psychology, as Mr. Rescher formulates it, seems to have a large assignment. According to him, this view denies that some perceptual properties of wholes are emergent. We may infer, then, that one who holds the view claims that no perceptual properties are emergent and consequently must show that all such properties can be deduced from description of parts plus a psychological theory. I wonder just which psychological theorists Mr. Rescher thinks are making this anti-Gestalt claim. The Gestalters bridge a long time span and theories opposing theirs have been many—Wundtian, structuralism, act psychology, contemporary S-R reinforcement theory, and non-reinforcement theory, etc. I think both Mr. Rescher and the Gestalters would find it difficult to show, say, that the S-R reinforcement theorists claim that *all* perceptual properties of wholes can be predicted from the description of their parts plus such notions as $S^HR$, D, etc.

Mr. Rescher utilizes the analysis of "emergence" formulated by Hempel and Oppenheim. I have not challenged the correctness of this analysis. Their formulation aims to eliminate the notion of absolute emergence by showing that emergence is only relative to some theory, and to prevent the notion of emergence from becoming vacuous—as it would, e.g., if it were a property of parts when suitably combined to produce wholes possessing certain properties—by requiring a statement of parts and attributes characterizing them. In this chapter, as a matter of fact, I urge the first of these points against Koffka's claim that "H, $H_2$, and $H_2O$ have all different properties which cannot be derived by *adding* properties of H's and O's." I argued that it is an insufficient view of emergence to claim that one cannot predict one set of properties from another; I claim that emergence means an inability to predict a future set of conditions from a previous set plus some theory. The important thing is that, given this meaning, I did not claim that some specified property, whose status is in doubt, is or is not emergent relative to other specified properties and theories. I raised no issue about what is or is not emergent, as Mr. Rescher does in psychology, but considered the meaning of "emergence" in any case. To determine what is or is not emergent is the scientist's task, an interesting one, to be sure, but, for all that, not the philosopher's.

*CHAPTER TWO*

## Isomorphism

1. E. G. Boring, "Psychophysiological Systems and Isomorphic Relations," *Psychological Review*, 43 (1936), pp. 565ff.; and R. W. Erickson, "Isomorphism as a Necessary Concept," *Journal of General Psychology*, 26 (1942), pp. 353ff.

2. Morris R. Cohen and Ernest Nagel, *An Introduction to Logic and Scientific Method* (New York: Harcourt, Brace and Company, 1934), p. 139.

3. Cf. E. G. Boring, *Sensation and Perception in the History of Experimental Psychology* (New York: D. Appleton-Century Co., 1942), pp. 34ff., 50. Cf. particularly, p. 37.

4. *Ibid.*, p. 89.

5. Further, Boring points out that the number of physical dimensions which a stimulus may have places no restriction on the total number of attributes a sensation may have, although it does restrict the number of *independent* attributes. Take the case where the physical stimulus is bi-dimensional and yields four sensory attributes. Suppose the functions relating each of the sensory attributes to the two dimensions of the stimulus are found through experimentation. Knowing these functions we would need only to know values of two sensory attributes in order to determine the values of the dimensions of the physical stimulus and finally to determine the other sensory attributes. The minimum number of sensory attributes which must be known, in addition to the functions, in order to determine all the rest of the sensory attributes, are in this sense *independent;*

and the number of independent attributes depends on the number of dimensions of the physical stimulus. As Boring concludes concerning Stevens' experimental results to which I have referred:

> The conclusion is that the [total] number of attributes of sensation is independent of the number of dimensions of the . . . stimulus. A bidimensional stimulus may yield a sensation with one or with $n$ attributes. The sensation will also be bidimensional in the sense that any two of its attributes will then determine all the others. . . . [*Philosophy of Science*, 2 (1935), p. 243.]

In such cases the only one-to-one relation that could possibly exist is between a complete set of sensory attributes, on the one hand, and the complete set of physical dimensions that determine them, on the other.

6. E.g., in the theories of Johannes Mueller and Julius Bernstein.

7. *Gestalt theory* is much more comprehensive than a psychological theory; it is also an epistemology and metaphysics.

8. Wolfgang Köhler, *Gestalt Psychology* (New York: Liveright, 1947), pp. 6off.

9. Boring, *Sensation and Perception in the History of Experimental Psychology,* pp. 88-89.

10. Köhler, *op. cit.,* p. 60.

11. *Ibid.,* p. 61.

12. *Ibid.*

13. *Ibid.,* pp. 61-63.

14. Köhler, *Dynamics in Psychology* (New York: Liveright, 1940), p. 55.

15. Köhler, *Gestalt Psychology,* p. 61.

16. Köhler, *The Place of Value in a World of Facts* (New York: Liveright, 1938), p. 251.

17. Köhler, *Dynamics in Psychology,* pp. 49ff.

18. Cf. footnote 1.

19. Cf. Köhler, *Gestalt Psychology,* p. 57; and Kurt Koffka, *Prin-*

*ciples of Gestalt Psychology* (New York: Harcourt, Brace and Co., 1935), pp. 61ff.

20. Cf. Köhler, *Gestalt Psychology*, p. 57; and Koffka, *op. cit.* pp. 61ff.

21. Koffka, *op. cit.*, pp. 33, 35.

22. *Ibid.*, p. 35.

23. *Ibid.*, p. 29.

24. Köhler,*The Place of Value in a World of Facts*, p. 108. Cf. Köhler, *Gestalt Psychology*, pp. 22ff.

25. Köhler, *The Place of Value in a World of Facts*, p. 109.

26. *Ibid.*, pp. 140-41.


### CHAPTER THREE
# Lawfulness

1. Kurt Koffka, *Principles of Gestalt Psychology* (New York: Harcourt, Brace and Co., 1935), p. 34.

2. *Ibid.*, pp. 27-28.

3. *Ibid.*, pp. 32-33.

4. *Ibid.*, p. 34. Cf. Chapter VI in *Principles of Gestalt Psychology.*

5. Cf. Gustav Bergmann, "Psychoanalysis and Experimental Psychology," *Mind*, 52 (1943), pp. 122-40. Reprinted in M. Marx, *Psychological Theory* (New York: The Macmillan Co., 1951), pp. 362-63.

6. Kenneth W. Spence, "The Nature of Theory Construction in Contemporary Psychology," *Psychological Review*, 51 (1944), pp. 47-68. Reprinted in Marx, *op. cit.*, cf. p. 75.

7. I use Clark Hull's learning theory as a paradigm, but Skinner's, Guthrie's, etc., would do as well as far as the present point is concerned. Cf. E. H. Madden, "The Nature of Psychological Explanation," *Methodos*, 9 (1957).

8. Wolfgang Köhler, *Gestalt Psychology* (New York: Liveright, 1947), p. 139.

9. *Ibid.*, pp. 141-42.

10. Max Wertheimer, in W. D. Ellis, *Source Book of Gestalt Psychology* (New York: The Humanities Press, 1950), pp. 71-88. See, e.g., pp. 86-87.

11. Koffka, *op. cit.*, pp. 58-61.

12. Kenneth W. Spence, "The Differential Response in Animals to Stimuli Varying Within a Single Dimension," *Psychological Review*, 44 (1937), pp. 430-44. There is some doubt today about this derivation, but even if it is unsuccessful it does not follow that no relational responses are learned.

13. Köhler, *op. cit.*, Chapters 8 and 9.

14. *Ibid.*, p. 162.

15. *Ibid.*

16. *Ibid.*, pp. 161-62.

17. *Ibid.*, p. 166.

18. *Ibid.*, p. 164.

19. Cf. D. Snygg, "The Need for a Phenomenological System of Psychology," *Psychological Review*, 48 (1941), pp. 404-24; and Robert S. Woodworth, *Contemporary Schools of Psychology*, Revised Ed. (New York: The Ronald Press Company, 1948), pp. 249-52, for "The 'Understanding' Psychology." *Verstehende* psychologists like Wilhelm Dilthey and Edouard Spranger not only emphasize the empathy viewpoint but also stress the *uniqueness* of human events in contrast to the *repeatable* events of the physical world. Andre Maurois, in his *Aspects of Biography* (Cambridge, 1929), stresses this point and applies it to history and biography. According to Maurois, the historian or biographer is like a portrait painter; his goal is to create a likeness of an individual. And in his concern with the individual and the instantaneous he is unlike the scientist who deals with general repeatable phenomena. "If we have not clearly observed what

happens when sodium and water are brought together, we have simply to begin again and watch more closely the second time. But the proper function of biography is to deal with the individual and the instantaneous" (p. 86). Inasmuch as the biographer deals with unique experiences, which we can never behold again, he cannot use the scientific method (*loc. cit.*).

However Maurois' view that science deals with general repeatable phenomena while biography, *like all history,* concerns the unique, the individual, and the instantaneous—essentially Windelband's old distinction between the nomothetic and the idiographic—is an oversimplified dichotomy. Physics, for example, is not independent of singular statements, those which refer to individual objects and events. In prediction one uses not only laws but initial conditions—say, the description of the state of a particular system at a particular time. And the prediction itself refers to another such state. Further, the only evidence that one has for a law is its exemplifications in particular systems. Conversely, biography is not free from general statements, those which refer to repeatable phenomena; namely, the behavioral maxims of everyday life and, depending on their degree of verification, the universal hypotheses or laws of psychology. Maxims, universal hypotheses, and laws are used both in establishing biographical facts and in explaining how they occurred.

Consider, as an example of the former, Lytton Strachey's discussion of the Rousseau affair (*Books and Characters,* New York, 1922, pp. 203-15). The Encyclopaedists insisted that Rousseau was a villain. Madame d'Epinay's *Memoirs* confirmed this view. The original manuscript of the *Memoirs,* however, reveals corrections and notes in the handwriting of Diderot and Grimm. Apparently the *Memoirs* is not an independent confirmation of the Encyclopaedists' view but was altered to conform to it. Did Diderot and Grimm conspire to disgrace and humiliate Rousseau? No, Strachey argues. From all we know of Diderot from other sources, he was a fearless and noble man, and these traits are incompatible with conspiracy. Strachey's argument is a first order enthymeme. The major premise "Noble men do not conspire," although not explicit, is an essential part of the argument. One does not have to make it explicit because it is obvious. This obviousness and consequent suppression of the maxims of everyday life, which figure prominently in biographical explanation, probably help to produce the illusion that general statements play no role in historical and biographical inference.

Among the universal hypotheses or laws of psychology that the biographer uses in explaining aspects of his subject's personality those of psychoanalysis figure prominently. Strachey, for example, in explaining James Anthony Froude's attachment to Carlyle, and his consequent moralizing in the *History of England,* writes,

> Old Mr. Froude had drawn a magic circle round his son, from which escape was impossible; and the creature whose life had been almost ruined by his father's moral cruelty . . . remained, in fact, in secret servitude—a disciplinarian, a Protestant, even a churchgoer, to the very end.

> When his father had vanished, [Froude] submitted himself to Carlyle. The substitution was symptomatic; the new father expressed in explicit dogma the unconscious teaching of the old. . . .
> (*Portraits in Miniature,* New York, 1931, pp. 193-94.)

This argument is another first order enthymeme. The law or universal hypothesis itself is not expressed; only its application to the particular case is made explicit. This procedure is usually followed when psychological laws are used in biographical explanation and, again, helps account for the illusion that biography and history are independent of general statements.

While there is in fact little explicit reference to psychological laws in biographical explanations, there is frequent reference to psychological "causes." The use of causal terminology, however, is a reliable sign that the explanation is enthymematic in nature. Causal explanations are usually applications of laws to individual events without an explicit formulation of the law which is a necessary condition for this application. This evidential problem must not be confused with the problem of the meaning of 'cause.' Whether 'cause' means nothing more than 'law' or involves, in addition, a compulsion between individual events, is a further question. Whatever the answer to it, a law whether expressed or not is still a necessary condition for asserting a causal relation between individual events.

There are, of course, many practical difficulties when the biographer uses psychological "causes" or laws to explain his subject's behavior. Maurois is quite right in insisting on them. No one is keeping a record of Bertrand Russell's dreams or Kurt Goedel's endocrine secretions so that the universal hypotheses of psychoanalysis and endocrinology may be used in explaining their behavior. Nevertheless where there are records to which psychological concepts are applicable it would be fatuous not to use them in explaining a subject's behavior.

Even though biography is not independent of general statements, either explicit or implicit, and singular ones do have a place in physics, we must not infer that Maurois' uniqueness argument is altogether misleading. The biographer *is* interested in individual events and is not himself seeking laws as is the scientist. In the explanation of individual events, it is true, he relies on laws, universal hypotheses, and maxims. However, these are not a result of his own investigations but are drawn from other areas, psychology and everyday life. In this respect biography is similar to geophysics. The geophysicist does not seek "geophysical laws" but tries to apply the laws of physics to the concrete course of physical events and so explain them.

The geophysics analogy is misleading, too, of course, because the geophysicist is interested simply in explaining phenomena while the biographer is interested in this and something else as well: he wants to satisfy the aesthetic interests of his readers. For the reader of biography the re-creation and reliving of past events has a charm all its own whether or not the events are explained. And this experience is a fundamental aesthetic value in biography. Still this aesthetic experience is not incompatible with an interest in explanation—which, indeed, has its own aesthetic value.

20. Snygg, *op. cit.*, pp. 404-24; and Woodworth, *op. cit.*

21. Cf. Theodore Abel, "The Operation Called 'Verstehen'," *American Journal of Sociology,* 54 (1948-49), pp. 211-18. Reprinted in

E. H. Madden, *The Structure of Scientific Thought* (Boston: Houghton Mifflin Co., 1960), pp. 158-66.

22. Cf. Andre Maurois, *op. cit.*

23. Theodore Abel, *op. cit.,* in Madden volume, p. 164.

*CHAPTER FOUR*

## Psychoanalytic Propositions

1. Cf. Sidney Hook., ed., *Psychoanalysis, Scientific Method, and Philosophy* (New York: New York University Press, 1959).

2. Morris Lazerowitz, "The Relevance of Psychoanalysis to Philosophy" in Hook, *op. cit.,* pp. 133-56.

3. Cf. E. H. Madden, "Psychoanalysis and Moral Judgeability," *Philosophy and Phenomenological Research,* 18 (1957).

4. Ernest Nagel, "Methodological Issues in Psychoanalytic Theory," in Hook, *op. cit.,* p. 43.

5. *Ibid.*

6. Cf. Francis Gramlich, "On the Structure of Psychoanalysis," in Hook, *op. cit.,* p. 298.

7. Sidney Hook, "Science and Mythology in Psychoanalysis," in Hook, *op cit.,* p. 214.

8. Jacob Arlow, "Psychoanalysis as Scientific Method," in Hook, *op. cit.,* p. 208.

9. *Ibid.,* p. 210.

10. Hook, *op. cit.,* p. 217.

11. Arthur C. Danto, "Meaning and Theoretical Terms in Psychoanalysis," in Hook, *op. cit.,* pp. 317-18.

12. Cf. Kenneth Spence, "Historical and Modern Conceptions of Psychology," in his *Behavior Theory and Conditioning* (New Haven: Yale University Press, 1956). Reprinted in E. H. Madden, *The Structure of Scientific Thought* (Boston: Houghton Mifflin Co., 1960). Cf. particularly pp. 143-46.

13. Cf. E. H. Madden, *The Structure of Scientific Thought,* pp. 10-11.

14. Arlow, *op. cit.,* p. 208.

15. Cf. Wesley C. Salmon, "Psychoanalytic Theory and Evidence," in Hook, *op. cit.,* p. 264.

16. Cf. John Hospers, "Philosophy and Psychoanalysis," in Hook, *op. cit.,* pp. 339-40.

17. Salmon, *op. cit.,* p. 261.

18. *Ibid.,* pp. 262-63.

19. Nagel, *op. cit.,* pp. 48-49.

20. *Ibid.*

21. *Ibid.,* p. 52

22. *Ibid.,* p. 49.

23. *Ibid.*

24. *Ibid.,* p. 52.

25. *Ibid.,* p. 53.

26. Cf. C. J. Ducasse, "Psychoanalysis and Suggestion: Metaphysics and Temperament," in Hook, *op. cit.,* pp. 319-23.

27. Cf. Chauncey Wright, "The Logic of Evolutionary Theory," in *The Philosophical Writings of Chauncey Wright,* ed. Edward H. Madden (New York: Liberal Arts Press, 1958), pp. 28-42.

28. Cf. Hospers, *op. cit.,* p. 340.

29. Cf. Gail Kennedy, "Psychoanalysis: Protoscience and Metapsychology," in Hook, *op. cit.,* p. 274.

30. Arlow, *op. cit.,* p. 204.

31. *Ibid.,* p. 206.

32. *Ibid.,* pp. 206-207.

33. Lawrence S. Kubie, "Psychoanalysis and Scientific Method," in Hook, *op. cit.,* pp. 63-64.

34. *Ibid.,* p. 64.

35. Cf. Kennedy, *op. cit.,* pp. 275-76.

36. Cf. Hartmann's, Kubie's and Arlow's essays in Hook, *op. cit.*

37. Heinz Hartmann, "Psychoanalysis as a Scientific Theory," in Hook, *op. cit.,* p. 9.

38. Nagel, *op. cit.,* p. 47.

39. *Ibid.*

40. Arthur Pap, "On the Empirical Interpretation of Psychoanalytic Concepts," in Hook, *op. cit.,* p. 295.

41. *Ibid.*

42. *Ibid.*

43. Cf. the discussion of this point in Chapter I of the present book.

44. Cf. K. MacCorquodale and P. E. Meehl, "On a Distinction Between Hypothetical Constructs and Intervening Variables," *Psychological Review,* 55 (1948), pp. 95-107.

45. *Ibid.*

46. Kenneth W. Spence, "The Differential Response in Animals to Stimuli Varying Within a Single Dimension," *Psychological Review,* 44 (1937), pp. 430-44.

CHAPTER FIVE

## Psychoanalysis and Responsibility

1. Lucius Garvin, *A Modern Introduction to Ethics* (Boston: Houghton Mifflin Co., 1953), p. 75.

2. The controversy between John Hospers and Herbert Fingarette is instructive at this point. Cf. John Hospers, "Free-Will and Psychoanalysis" in W. Sellars and J. Hospers, eds., *Readings in Ethical Theory* (New York: Appleton-Century-Crofts, Inc., 1952), pp. 560-75; and Herbert Fingarette, "Psychoanalytic Perspectives on Moral Guilt and Responsibility: A Re-evaluation," *Philosophy and Phenomenological Research,* XVI (1955), pp. 18-36. This controversy is an interesting one to analyze.

Hospers claims that one cannot legitimately be held responsible for the inevitable consequences of uncontrollable events (i.e., for the queer or criminal behavior which results from adult neuroses, which result from childhood neuroses, over the formation of which the individual obviously had no control). Fingarette denies this claim and, in addition, attacks what he takes to be another blunder in the philosophical interpretation of psychoanalysis, namely, that neurotic guilt is not real guilt. I suspect this conflict results mainly from confusions to which each author, perhaps, has contributed a share.

Therapy, Fingarette says, often consists, first, in making the patient aware that he feels intensely guilty. The second step is to find the ground of the guilt feeling which, in neurosis, is unconscious. The analyst tries to reduce, only *temporarily,* the burden of felt guilt so that the wish, to which the guilt is attached, finally comes into consciousness. The crucial point is that the patient rightly feels guilt over the wish. The guilt feeling is not disproportionate; the wish merits it. In the cases where the wish looks trivial it is, by and large, a mask that a fundamentally evil wish, which is unconscious, wears. And it is fruitless to say that the person is not really guilty because after all he did not *act* on his wish; for the wish itself is *morally,* albeit not consequentially, equivalent to the act. Consequently, the first step in therapy, when the guilt feeling becomes conscious, can be described morally by saying "the patient is enabled to face his guilt rather than to run away from it as he has in the past" (p. 27). And when the ground of the guilt, the evil wish, emerges into consciousness one can say, from the moral perspective, that the person has been forced to face not only his guilt but in addition the evil within him which is the basis of his guilt.

At this point in therapy the patient is able to reflect upon his evil wish in the context of his life circumstances and ideals, which context, through therapy, he sees more realistically than before. Appraising his wish within this context, he is at last able to reject the wish, modify it, or retain it, and even sometimes modify one of his fundamental ideals. As a result of therapy, then, the patient *accepts* responsibility; i.e., accepts as *his* the task of doing something about his wishes or suffering the moral and psychological consequences. "In spite of Hospers' assumption that we cannot be held responsible for the inevitable consequences of uncontrollable events, we seem to see in therapy an acceptance of responsibility for just such events" (p. 30). And this result unexpectedly lends support to the existentialist analysis of moral responsibility. It is not that we *were* or *are* responsible, as the existentialist says, but we must *accept* responsibility, by an act of will, of deliberate choice, as the price of maturity. True, it is hard to be responsible in the future for some of the things we are when we had no hand in so becoming, but nevertheless we must accept the hard reality that the world is not fair and just and assume responsibility in order sensibly to go about the business of living. Stop complaining; you are paying the price of no longer being a child. We can reach true humanity only by accepting the challenge to *make* the world just.

(1) *Guilt.* Clearly, I think, it is one thing to say an agent's wish or act is guilty in the sense that it is condemnable or morally wrong and another to say that the agent is guilty in the sense that *he* is condemnable. The second sense of "guilty" is the usual one, the sense which presupposes responsibility, and occurs in legal sentences like "not guilty by reason of insanity." Fingarette realizes that his use of "guilty" does not presuppose responsibility—we can be guilty when not responsible, he says, because guilt occurs very early in life, while responsibility occurs later—yet he blurs the distinction by going from "guilty wish" to "guilty agent" before responsibility occurs. The first step in therapy, when the guilt feeling becomes conscious, he writes, can be described morally by saying, "the patient is enabled to face his guilt rather than to run away from it as he has in the past" (p. 27). This type of blur occurs frequently; but it is not the confusion which leads to his dissent from Hospers' view.

(2) *Responsibility.* I can see no objection whatever in saying man *becomes* responsible or *accepts* responsibility as the price of maturity; and consequently that he does accept responsibility for the inevitable consequences of his personality and character even though they were not under his formative control. This claim effectively helps to meet the determinist's original di-

lemma. The point is, however, that in neurotic behavior this result only occurs after therapy. The forensic psychiatrist, on the other hand, is claiming that prior to therapy, or where therapy has not occurred or is unsuccessful, the "malevolent unconscious" makes an agent nonresponsible for his behavior; and we have seen above the type of reason he gives to defend this view. Hospers in some places in his article seems to be making the same point. However, if this is the case then his and Fingarette's views could not conflict because they do not even meet on the same ground; yet Fingarette offers his view as a devastating criticism of Hospers'. The only way to explain this state of affairs is that Fingarette interprets Hospers' view as if it were the traditional determinist's point that all behavior is nonresponsible because it is determined by our character but we did not have any control over *its* formation. That Fingarette interprets Hospers thusly is again suggested when Fingarette says that Hospers' analysis of psychoanalysis is not necessary or needed to make the point.

> It is interesting to note that we would indeed have a paradox, if we accept Hospers' assumption about moral responsibility. For in that case, even if we did not consider psychoanalytic doctrine but simply granted that, in some way or other, our present nature and behavior are the causal consequences of earlier states of the world, we would be faced with the problem of explaining how we could *ever* be responsible for *any* of our adult behavior. (P. 31.)

In view of some of Hospers' statements, Fingarette's interpretation seems legitimate; or understandable, at any rate, even if Hospers did not intend to hold the view. Hospers writes, for example: "An act is free when it is determined by the man's character, say moralists; but what if the most decisive aspects of his character were already irrevocably acquired before he could do anything to mold them?" (p. 563). "The unconscious is the master of every fate and the captain of every soul" (p. 572). Also Fingarette's interpretation is suggested in the way in which Hospers presents his analysis of psychoanalysis as if it were a necessary refutation of the Schlick-Russell type of dissolution of the determinism-responsibility issue when it is an (elaborate?) sufficient one. And bringing in the issue of the nonresponsibility of non-neurotic unconscious behavior I suspect is misleading, too, because it brings up additional issues to which Fingarette's and existential analyses are highly pertinent.

Hospers and Fingarette, it seems to me, each in his own way, slide psychiatry into the traditional determinism-responsibility issue; Hospers suggesting, in one way or another, that psychoanalysis reinforces determinism and Fingarette unequivocally holding that it reinforces commonsensical self-determinism and so moral responsibility. This maneuver, I believe, is unfortunate either way; and the real import of psychoanalysis for morality—namely, that neurotic behavior is not morally judgeable—is likely to be lost in the resulting confusion. The forensic psychiatrist cannot be anything but dismayed at this turn of events.

3. Fingarette, *op. cit.;* Stephen Toulmin, "The Logical Status of Psycho-analysis" in M. Macdonald, ed., *Philosophy and Analysis* (Oxford: Basil Blackwell, 1954), pp. 132-39; and Anthony Flew, "Psycho-analytic Explanation" in *Philosophy and Analysis,* pp. 139-48. Toulmin and Flew follow F. Waismann's distinction in "Language Strata" in A. G. N. Flew, ed., *Logic and Language, Second Series* (Oxford: Basil Blackwell, 1953), pp. 1-13.

4. Toulmin and Flew.

5. Gregory Zilboorg, *The Psychology of the Criminal Act and Punishment* (London: Hogarth Press, 1955), pp. 25-27. Other men whose work is particularly important in this area, and from whom I have profited greatly, are Winfred Overholser and Walter Bromberg.

6. *Ibid.,* pp. 71-72.

7. *Ibid.,* p. 32.

8. *Ibid.,* p. 126.

9. *Ibid.,* pp. 119ff.

10. Cf. David W. Louisell, "Review of Zilboorg's *The Psychology of the Criminal Act and Punishment,*" *Scientific Monthly,* 79 (July-December, 1954), pp. 332-33.

11. Zilboorg, *op. cit.,* pp. 28-29.

12. Jerome Hall, "Science and Reform in Criminal Law" in Philip Wiener, ed., *Readings in Philosophy of Science* (New York: Charles Scribner's Sons, 1953), pp. 297-309. Text and footnotes.

13. Zilboorg, *op. cit.*, pp. 112-13.

14. *Ibid.*, pp. 118-19.

# Index

# INDEX

## Index